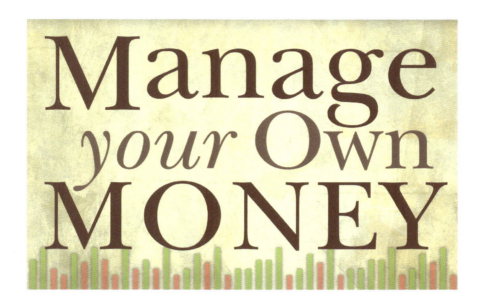

A nuts and bolts guide for the do-it-yourself investor and investment professionals

By Daniel J. Clemons

ISBN: 1-4392-0211-7
ISBN-13: 9781439202111

Visit www.booksurge.com to order additional copies.

TABLE OF CONTENTS

FORWARD

No Path to Prosperity would be complete without learning how to become a millionaire. It just doesn't happen overnight or by accident. As an incentive to spend some time with each page, you will find ways of becoming a millionaire throughout the book. My technology to manage money was 15 years in the making. Upon its completion in 2002, I sold it to other financial professionals and Registered Investment Advisors. Before you fast forward to the Predictor, the new technologies that manage money, or portfolio construction, I would like to discuss the many causes of financial failure. You can never be wealthy if you can't control your budget, so a brief discussion on spending is a must. Budgets and retirement planning are intertwined. Balance Sheets only take a few minutes and will become your annual report card. People spend a lot of valuable time trying to pick a good mutual fund. Why not have really good top performing mutual funds pick you? I'll make it easy for you to pick mutual fund portfolios with promise! How many horses will you need to pull your financial wagon? What are some of the mistakes amateur investors make? Managing money does not have to be rocket science if you will follow a few simple rules. In fact, it is much easier than you think. Can the direction of the stock market be predicted? My Predictor says it can. Does Technical Analysis really work? We'll soon find out. No personal money management course can be called complete if it does not make you aware of conflicts of interest between you and the institutions that hold your money.

Using this technology, managing your retirement assets will be made easier. How much income will my retirement assets produce? In the pages that follow, I will share some simple math that can help pave your path to financial independence for an early and carefree retirement. I would like to save you some money by making you a savvy insurance buyer. Last but not least, we'll discuss Will and Trust planning. Are you sure your trust does everything you want it to do? We shall see shortly. Essentially, everything important to know about money will be discussed. All my best-kept secrets about the management of money are in this book.

After a 30-year career in the financial services industry working as a Certified Financial Planner and Registered Investment Advisor, I am ready to help you learn to **Manage Your Own Money**. I am retired and have no economic ties with any company or financial institution. My advice is independent of outside influence. My legacy is not the many clients I worked for throughout my career nor my technology that manages money but the hundreds of high school seniors that take my Personal Money Management Course each year. I am frequently asked to do a class for adults. Instead, it is to you this book is dedicated.

Chapter 1

FIGHTING FINANCIAL FAILURE

Avoiding financial potholes along the road of life is vital if you want to achieve financial success. I don't want to see you trip, stumble and fall and skin your financial nose. Words that best describe financial failure all begin with the letter D.

Debt – Bankruptcy is the end result of excessive amounts of debt. I never understood why anyone would want to pay 20% more for everything they purchase by handing a clerk their credit card. One hard fast rule in my financial house is that **all credit cards have to be paid in full at the end of every month. <u>There are no exceptions.</u>** I never paid a penny of credit card interest and I am not about to start now. Shoppers want to get a bargain on sale and then finance the purchase by using a credit card. How dumb can that be? Debt is more than a speed bump on the road to financial riches; it's a cement roadblock. With the exception of your home mortgage and educational expenses, you should be debt free before investing.

Discretionary Spending – is choosing to spend on nonessentials because you want it rather than on something you really need. A side affect of over spending in the discretionary department is when you have too much month at the end of the money. To become wealthy you have to **save money** instead of **spending money** on things that are not needed and rarely used. You show me a person with a spending problem and I'll show you a person who has no budget.

Divorce – Dividing your estate in half is not the end of the world if you are young, but when divorce happens late in life it can be disastrous. Returning to work may very well be your only option if you are retired. It is a severe setback and should be avoided.

Drugs – Even tobacco is an expensive drug that should be avoided. Smoke two packs a day and you have a $300 a month habit. Invest that $300 a month for 30 years and you add $365,991.31 to your net worth. The choice is to smoke and risk your health or you can add $25,619.39 to your retirement income.

Detention – You don't want to call D-block home under any circumstances. There is no money to be made behind bars.

Death or Disability – Insurance can guarantee you protection against these two financial risks. In the absence of insurance, loss of income means not enough money available to fund your monthly budget.

Dependents – It can take more than $100,000 to raise a child to age 18. Raising too many children might require moving in with your children so they can take care of you. There is no doubt about it; family size is an important issue when it comes to economic net worth.

The 10%
Path to Prosperity

If a 35-year old person with a $50,000 annual income budgets $45,000 for expenditures and $5,000 for savings, he or she can be a millionaire at 65!! At 8% interest, $416.67 a month grows to $620,988.02 in 30 years. With a 3% raise in pay each year, that figure swells to $1,168,559.10 paying out $81,798.48 at age 65! The idea here is to pay yourself first at the beginning of every month.

Chapter 2

BALANCED BUDGETS
BUILD WEALTH

Matching income with expenditures is challenging for just about everyone and impossible for the poor. Just talking about limiting your spending can be a big first step toward building personal wealth. There is no set time of year to craft a budget and you can do as many as you like as often as you like. Talking about limiting your discretionary spending gets a couple on the same page working for the same goal: to save more money. It's those face-to-face meetings that are remembered when you are in the stores trying to decide whether or not to make a purchase. If you are going to create wealth you must spend less than you make. It is as simple as that. Often we think we need to buy something when we really don't. We buy things we can't use and all too often refuse to return unused items to the store. It is not easy at first to rein in spending. However, once you get spending under control, running a tight budget will become easier as you get used to living on less.

There are two basic types of spending, Discretionary and Non-discretionary. Non-discretionary items like housing, heat, and electricity can't easily be changed. There is little you can do to reduce the cost of transportation or soaring medical costs. On the other hand, discretionary spending on such items as vacations, entertainment, and eating out can be changed. You can use spending caps to limit spending on such things as Christmas, birthdays, and charitable contributions. Cash allowances for discretionary spending must be capped. Domestic help around the house is a luxury, as are grounds keepers. Pitch in and do some, if not all, the work yourself and save.

Publications lie around unread; do you really need all those magazines? With a little planning, you can save on the high cost of gas by using the shortest route to the stops you need to make. When it comes to buying clothes, just buy what you need. Drive down the cost of the family car by driving it longer. Your cost per mile goes down by putting more miles on your present cars odometer.

I have always felt that if you can't pay cash for it you have not earned the right to have whatever it is. Debt is a very high tax for buying something. There are only two types of debt that make sense to me and they are mortgage debt and educational debt. Owning your own home is preferred over renting and some of the best property you can own is intellectual property. Advancing your career in order to make more money is a good use of capital. If all I could afford was a 1986 Honda Civic paid in full then that is what you would find in my garage. I have not and will not finance a car. Zero financing just means they have added the interest into the price of the car. Pay cash for everything and you will turn your financial life around. Life's luxuries will come to those who don't have to have it all right now. Interest paid on debt is money down a rat hole. Debt makes lenders rich and borrowers poor. The single biggest improvement one can make is to eliminate debt. One of my associates wrote on his business card, "Living the debt free life style." Retirees know that debt free means you have more money to spend. Debt is a heavy financial burden on governments, corporations, and individuals. If you don't own it, the lender can take it away from you. The single biggest improvement you can make to your financial health is to eliminate your debt.

The following budget sheet will help you total your expenditures.

AN EASY TO USE BUDGET SHEET

Housing

    monthly payment   _____

    property taxes   _____

    associations   _____

    insurance   _____

    repairs   _____

    lawn care   _____

    other   _____

Short term Credit (1yr)

    Visa   _____

    Master Card   _____

    Discover card   _____

    Am Express   _____

    Bank loans   _____

    other   _____

    other   _____

Transportation

    gas & oil   _____

    maintenance   _____

    insurance   _____

    license fee   _____

    rec vehicles   _____

Intermediate (2-10 yrs)

    auto 1   _____

    auto 2   _____

    time share   _____

    personal loan   _____

    education   _____

Food & Household

    groceries   _____

    eating out   _____

    maintenance   _____

    cleaning service   _____

    furnishings   _____

    pet care   _____

Personal Care

    clothes   _____

    hair care   _____

    spending $ _____

    hobbies   _____

    memberships   _____

    other   _____

Medical

    health costs   _____

    dental costs   _____

    optical costs   _____

Gifts

    Christmas   _____

    birthday   _____

    anniversary   _____

Insurance Premiums		Recreation	
life	_____	movies	_____
disability	_____	vacation	_____
major med	_____	camping	_____
liability	_____	weekend trips	_____
other	_____	memberships	_____

Contributions		Publications	
church	_____	newspaper	_____
vets/goodwill	_____	magazines	_____
societies	_____	journals	_____
other	_____	other	_____

Utilities		Union Dues	_____
gas & electric	_____		
telephone	_____	Other Services	
water	_____	_____	_____
cable TV	_____	_____	_____
Internet	_____		
Cell Phone	_____		

Never ask of money spent
Where the spender thinks it went.
Nobody was ever meant
To remember or invent
What he did with every cent.
–Robert Frost

Budgets Build Better Balance Sheets

Shrinking the size of your budget is the single most significant step you can take towards building a stronger and more pristine balance sheet. You can never be wealthy if you can't live on less than you make.

A Smarter Home Mortgage
A Path to Prosperity

Paying extra on a 30-year mortgage is a very smart thing to do. The mortgage payment on $250,000 at 6.25% interest is $1,539.29 per month. Mortgage interest totals $304,145.48 over the life of a 30-year mortgage. Increasing the monthly payment by 1/3; in this case $460.71; will reduce the interest paid to $155,328.84. This is a savings of $148,816.64 and it shortens the loan by 13.08 years!! Continue to save the $2,000 a month at 7% for 13 years and you will own a home, free and clear, plus have $506,661.59 invested in bonds. Your reward is monthly income of $2,955.53 for life!

Chapter 3

FEBRUARY'S BALANCE SHEET

Year-end statements from retirement plans, banks and brokerage accounts, make February the ideal time to complete a Balance Sheet. The Balance Sheet is so quick and so easy. All you need to do is add up everything you own and subtract everything you owe to arrive at your Net Worth. **Assets minus Liabilities equal Net Worth.** This becomes your Year-end report card. The Balance Sheet is a celebration of your year-over-year progress. It shows your **total growth rate**. Not only does it show the growth rate of all your investments combined but also the amount of money saved during the year. Employer contributions to a pension are part of that growth rate too. Any time you have a double-digit year-over-year growth rate, pat yourself on your back. The math is very easy to do. Subtracting last years total Net Worth from this year's total Net Worth gives you the amount your estate grew during the year. Stop right there and give your significant other a high five! To calculate the percentage increase year-over-year, divide the amount of growth you just calculated by last years Total Net Worth. For example, if last years Net Worth was $375,962.17 subtract this year's total of $442,325.87 and you get $66,363.70. Divide last years total Net Worth of $375,962.17 into $66,363.70 and you get 17.65%! It is not uncommon to see year-over-year growth rates of 10 to 25%! Personal savings and stock market sized returns can produce some pretty impressive numbers.

ASSETS MINUS LIABILITIES = NET WORTH

Liquid Assets

- Checking
- Savings accounts
- Emergency fund
- Money market account
- Cash

Investment Assets

- Stocks
- Bonds
- Real Estate
- Futures
- Precious Metals
- Collectibles

Retirement Assets

- IRAs
- Company Retirement Plans
- Annuities

Business Assets

- Inventory
- Land
- Goodwill

Personal Assets

- Residence
- Furnishings
- Vehicles
- Recreational Vehicles
- Other personal assets

Debt (Yikes!)

- Mortgage
- Credit Cards
- Auto Loans
- Personal Loans
- Educational Loans
- Family Loans
- Business Loans
- Line of Credit

Jay Leno's Personal Path to Prosperity

Who doesn't watch the Tonight Show with Jay Leno? Everyone needs a good laugh to end their day and no one does it better than Jay Leno. My guess is that Jay has not spent a lot of time studying the fine art of investing, but he did create for himself one of the best Paths to Prosperity that I have ever heard. Being a car guy's car guy, Jay was a guest on a TV car show I was watching. Jay made a financial statement so huge; it blew me clear across the room. Out of the clear blue Jay said, "I have never spent a penny of my NBC money." Slammed me into the wall, he did. Wow, get out of here! He has never spent a penny of his NBC money? I have no idea how much Jay currently makes but I had heard mentioned at one time 15 million dollars. No matter, Jay's Path to Prosperity was saving his NBC money. Jay went on to say, "My wife and I live on personal appearances, stand up comedy in Las Vegas, endorsements, and other televisions shows." I thought Jay's idea of living on one source of income and saving the other was a terrific idea! How many two-income households are there? How many could live on one income if they had to? How many people moonlight or have a second job? Way to go Jay!

Chapter 4

GETTING LONG THE MARKET

Real estate is where we live and Wall Street is where we make our money. Before I get to my Technology that Manages Money, I would like to share some reasons why we all need to become savvy investors. Let's take a look at the past investment performance of a few mutual funds posting some pretty tantalizing returns.

First, lets take a look at the Fairholme Fund FAIRX. According to Morningstar, in 2001 Fairholme was up 6.2%, down 1.6% in 2002, up 24% in 2004, up 13.7% in 2005, up 16.7% in 2006, and up 12.4% in 2007. Fairholme has an annualized return of 14.06% over the last 3 years and up 18.53% each year over the last 5 years.

Fidelity Leveraged Company FLVCX was up 3.2% in 2001, down 1.8% in 2002, up 96.3% in 2003, up 24.5% in 2004, up 17.5% in 2005, up 17.6% in 2006, and up 17.9% in 2007. The Fidelity Leveraged Company Fund has a 3-year annualized return of 18.95% and 5-year return of 26.38% per year.

The Metzler Payden European Emerging Markets Fund MPYMX was up 44.7% in 2003, up 53.2% in 2004, up 38% in 2005, up 46.3% in 2006, and up 28.5% in 2007. In the last 3 years the Metzler Payden European Emerging Markets Fund was up 34.55% per year and up 37.04% per year over the previous 5 years.

The CGM Focus Fund CGMFX has a high Standard Deviation but is well worth a closer look. The CGM Focus Fund was up 47.7% in 2001, down 17.8% in 2002, up 66.5% in 2003, up 12.4% in 2004, up 25.3% in 2005, up 14.9% in 2006, and up 80% in 2007. The CGM Focus Fund was up 37.78% over the last three years and up 37.65% in each of the last 5 years.

Last but not least is Harbor International HIINX up 40.3% in 2003, up 17.5% in 2004, up 20.3% in 2005, up 32.2% in 2006, and up 21.4% in 2007. Harbor International was up 25.45% in each of the last 3 years and up 26.1% annualized over the last 5 years.

There is one big problem with all these funds and that is few investors reading this book currently own or have owned these funds over the last 3 or 5 years. Don't feel bad because chances are good they have not showed up on your neighbor's radar screen either. **If you are going to get rich, you need to get "long the market" and stay there.** "Long the market" means you own shares of stock or stock mutual funds. Flat means you don't currently have a position in the market. I worry more about being flat and missing out on a recovery than I do being long and losing some of my profit.

Disclaimer – Just because I own these funds does not mean you should too. Past performance is no guarantee of future results. It is important to know your objective, risk tolerance, and time horizon so you won't trip, stumble and skin your financial nose. As with all mutual funds, call the fund companies and ask for an Investor Kit and read it carefully before deciding to invest or sending money. Mutual fund contact information such as an 800 number can easily be found on Morningstar.com. Just enter the symbol of the fund and click Purchase Info on the left.

The last point I want to make about these investment results is that the S&P 500 was down 23.37% in 2002. The market is a little like a rubber band stretched from point A to point B. The economy and international events can stretch it too far up or too far down. In time, it has always snapped back to equilibrium. Let's see if that is true. Let's review the 2002 results of the funds we just discussed one more time. They were down 1.6%, down 1.8%, down 17.8% and the S&P 500 was down 23.37% in 2002. Now let's take a look at what happened in 2003; up 24%, up 96.3%, up 66.5%, and up 40.3% based on the above funds we just talked about. The average of those four funds was down 11.14% in 2002. The average of the four funds was up 56.78% in 2003. The point is that the market does snap back to equilibrium over time. Savvy investors know that selling at market peaks and buying at market bottoms post the most profits!

🙶🙷

Chapter 5

INTRODUCING A NEW TECHNOLOGY TO MANAGE MONEY

My new technology that manages money came to me in bits and pieces over what seemed like a very long time, which felt like an eternity for me. Always experimenting, I wanted to know if a moving average had any predictability of future performance. The answer surprised me. I thought I was done inventing my technology that manages money in 2002 when The Predictor showed up at my financial front door quite by surprise in the summer of 2007. Like pieces of a puzzle, I found a piece that fits here and then I would find a piece that fits there. Never once did I wake up in the middle of the night with a bright new idea I just had to try. It was all roll up your sleeves hard work that seemed to go on day after day and month after month.

This chapter is not meant to be a Glossary of Investment terms or long boring meaningless paragraphs of nothing. I just want you to know just what you need to know so you can close this book and get on with your financial life. This book is intended to help you make better decisions about your money. Learning how to manage money well is what this chapter is all about. It is what this book is all about. It is what I am all about.

The Magic Inside Microsoft Money

Throughout my career financial software got better and better as it evolved over time. I used Money 2000 for a long time and now use Money 2003 to track all my investments. I tracked all my client investment accounts using Microsoft Money. I like the early versions of Microsoft Money because the software saves the investment data on my hard drive rather than Microsoft's website. Older versions of Microsoft Money Deluxe can be purchased on eBay for less than $10.

I am not a Microsoft Money aficionado so I am not an authority on newer versions of this really great piece of software. I don't use Quicken, but my guess is that you can set it up to do exactly what Microsoft Money does. The key is to set up a Total Return on Investment (ROI) moving average as shown below.

Once you have your current accounts set up in Microsoft Money, right click on the gray bar that says: Symbol, Name, and select **Customize Current View**. From there select **Portfolio Columns**. Over on the left side left click on **% change** and then press the **add** button. Select the following columns: Total Return 1-Week, Total Return 4-Week, Total Return 3-Month, and Total Return YTD or year to date and press the add button so each will be added to your Portfolio View. My column reads across: Symbol, Name, % Change, ROI 1-Week, ROI 4-Week, ROI 3-month, ROI YTD, Cost Basis, Market Value, Gain, % Portfolio, Last Price, Change, % of Portfolio, Total Quantity, Last Transaction. You can click and drag those columns anywhere you want but that is the order I prefer on my computer.

Symbol – Name - %Change – ROI 1-Week – ROI 4-Week – ROI 3-month – ROI YTD, etc.

Chapter 6

PICKING PORTFOLIOS WITH PROMISE

This one technology is worth the price of the book alone. A Watch List is nothing more than constructing a list of stocks or mutual funds you want to follow in Microsoft Money. In the Forward, I talked about having an investment select you. How to properly use a Watch List was one of my most prized discoveries. This is but one of my money management technologies that I sold to other Financial Advisors. I give it freely to my high school seniors and now it is yours to use.

The idea of a Watch List came to me at lunch with a sales representative one-summer day in 1988. While at lunch, I caught a glimpse of what looked like a list of mutual funds that were ranked by percentage in descending order. It was not shown to me but it caught my eye for a split second. As I recall, it was a list of Sector mutual funds, which focus on companies within the same industry such as technology, telecommunication, and transportation. What is that all about, I asked? Interesting very interesting, I thought. Almost instantly, I said to myself I must have that on my computer.

I used a Watch List for the longest of time without really knowing what it was telling me. However, I had pondered two very important questions.

Could a mutual fund's moving average have predictability and what can a Watch List do to improve returns? I experimented with a one week moving average, a two-week moving average, and averaged a one-week and a four-week together. I tried all kinds of combinations looking for predictability.

Calculating a percentage gain of a stock or mutual fund over the last 4-weeks is easily done. If the price of the fund was $24 thirty-one days ago we subtract that from today's price of $26.50 equaling $2.50 divided by $24 equals 10.41%. So the fund is said to be up 10.4% over the last 4-weeks. To make it a moving average, Microsoft Money does the calculation using two new numbers everyday.

Experiment I did with all kinds of combinations of moving average returns over different time periods and found that funds with the best **4-week moving average carried over to some of the best performing funds at the end of the year.** One day out of the clear blue I was sitting at my computer looking at my Mid Cap Watch List made up of medium sized companies when Money asked **me** a question, "Dan, do you really know what your are looking at?" I said, "I am looking at the Return on Investment (ROI) as a percentage up or percentage down over the last 4-weeks. What is so great about that, I asked myself? Then Money said, **"What you are looking at are portfolios of stock mutual funds and it is those stocks in those portfolios that make you money. The 4-week moving average is telling you what Wall Street thinks of that portfolio of stocks in light of current interest rates, sectors that are currently in favor, and economic conditions."**

Right then and there I knew I was onto something really important in my fund selection process. Let the Wall Street experts tell you which fund you should own. From that moment on, I relied on My Watch Lists to tell me which mutual fund manager had assembled the better portfolio. I am not saying that three and five year returns aren't an important proxy for a fund because I also require a fund to have doubled money, a 14.4% annualized return over the last five years just to make it onto my Watch List.

My requirements for inclusion on a Watch list are rather strict. My funds have to perform in the top 5% of their Morningstar Category and have doubled money over the last 5 years. The only exception to that rule is for my Growth and Income Watch List where a 14.4% return for inclusion is not required. I am not particular about which fund goes onto my Watch List because I know the best funds with the best performing portfolios will be at the top of all my Watch Lists.

So when I chose funds for my client accounts, they came off my **4-week Watch List**. You don't have to pick the number one fund because you might be looking for a fund with lower volatility or Standard Deviation. The objective is to be invested in a portfolio of stocks that are outperforming in real time right now. What happened three and five years ago has little to do with stocks currently in the portfolio. You don't have to figure out a funds investment style, value vs. growth, because the investment style Wall Street likes best will be listed in descending order right before your eyes.

You can have as many Watch Lists as you like. You can enter as many funds as you want on a Watch List. At the end of the day, the best performing funds will be at the top of that 4-week moving average. **You will be looking at the portfolio that Wall Street likes best.** You can click at the top of each of those moving averages columns and Microsoft Money will sort in descending order.

I have a Watch List for Stocks I want to follow, although I limit the amount of money, which limits my exposure to individual stocks primarily because of individual company risk. I don't care much for earnings surprises or when companies warn investors that the economy is adversely impacting their sales. Exchange traded ETFs eliminate company risk because they own a portfolio of stocks just like a mutual fund. They track better on stockcharts.com and I don't have to monitor them as closely as I do individual common stocks.

I have several mutual fund Watch Lists based on company size or capitalization. I have a Watch List for Large Cap, Mid Cap, Small Cap, Foreign, Sectors, ETFs, Conservative Growth and Income funds, and stocks. I do follow commodities but I have never cared much for precious metals.

Price per share can be updated daily at the push of a button. To add a fund to your Watch List just enter a **buy** for 100 shares of the fund at today's closing price found on Morningstar.com or Stockcharts.com. The percentage is the same no matter how many shares you enter so I just enter 100.

To actually purchase shares of a stock or mutual fund, you will need to call the fund company for an investor kit, know the funds risks, and fill out an application or you can purchase them through an IRA custodian such as Fiserv or Sterling or online brokerage account such as E*trade, Charles Schwab, or Scottrade.

During market corrections, a decline of up to 10% or less, the 4-week moving average will turn red showing the funds percentage loss over the last 4-weeks. What Wall Street is saying then is these are the portfolios' holding up the best in light of the economy, interest rates, and investor sentiment. These funds tend to not be the best performing at year-end. They are just the ones holding up well at the moment. If you want a fund in your portfolio that holds up well in a bear market, which is defined as two quarters of negative GDP or Gross Domestic Product, pick a fund doing well under adverse economic conditions.

෬෭

Chapter 7

FINDING FUNDS AT MORNINGSTAR.COM

I can't say enough about Morningstar.com especially when it comes to screening for mutual funds to put on your Watch List. Their premium services are becoming a tad bit expensive but you can get a substantial amount of free information just by looking around their website. Their predefined free fund screener will work just fine for most investors. With their basic subscription, you can enter your own criteria to screen for and fine top performing mutual funds. No top performing mutual fund can hide for long from my screens. Looking at 16,000 funds will drive you nuts so I like to skim off the top 5% ranked by performance within their category. Then I want to see who has been good enough to double shareholder money over the last five years. Make that cut and the mutual funds have earned the right to be on my Watch List, but **they have not earned the right to manage my money**. From there, I sit back and wait for the 4-week moving average to tell me which mutual fund portfolio Wall Street investors like best. They might have had a great portfolio 3 and 5 years ago but our performance driven financial minds want to know how they are doing right now. **Those funds with the best 4-week moving average tend to have the best performance at year-end.** Near the end of each year, I would tap at the top of the year-to-date column to sort my Watch List in descending order and to my surprise the best performing funds at year-end were still the best performing over the last 4-weeks. This discovery was a best-kept secret of mine for years. It gave me a big edge that set my practice apart from other financial advisors. My clients were always happy with their performance but never knew how it was done.

Morningstar also ranks mutual funds on a star system. They also list funds they like, which you can track on your Watch List. Morningstar makes finding funds for your Watch List easy. I subscribe to Morningstar's Premium Service so I can do more sophisticated screens than their Free Fund Screener, which will get new investors off to a great start. Here is how I find candidates for my Watch List on the Morningstar.com website:

My favorite Mutual Fund Screen

- Select Fund Category – All Domestic Stock or Intl Stock (9060)

- Trailing Return % rank in category – Select 12 month rank (1064) within category and then <= 5%

- Again Trailing Return % rank in category – Select 3-year (891) rank within category and then <=5%

- Again Trailing Return % rank in category – Select 3-months (29) rank within category and then <5%

Our search started by looking at 9060 mutual funds and ended up with 29 worthy candidates for your Watch List. You are welcome to put as many funds on your Watch List as you want. In the end, the best performing funds will select you.

The 50 By 40 Path to Prosperity

My goal in managing client accounts was to double their money every five years, which became almost impossible right after 9/11 but it was a worthy goal to be sure. Saving $50,000 by age 40 is a pretty popular Path to Prosperity among my high school seniors. Saving $138.20 monthly at age 25 with an 8.5% return will get you to $50,000 by age 40! Using mutual funds with higher returns will get you to this lofty goal even faster. Saving $50,000 by age 40 and then doubling it every five years will bring you to retirement in a hurry. At age 45, the account would be worth $100,000, by age 50 $200,000, by age 55 $400,000, by age 60 $800,000 and $1,600,000 at age 65. Using a 7% Distribution rate, the retirement income would total $112,000 a year for life without touching principal, as long as the account earned at least 7%.

One high school senior came up to me in class and said, "What if I can save $50,000 by age 25?" I could tell right away that age 40 was way over his financial horizon. I answered, "Then you will be retired on $112,000 per year at age 50. Oh, by the way, are you working? He answered, "No, but I'll have $50,000 by age 25!" One of the students asked Mr. Brian Cuilty, a Roseburg High School Economics Teacher, how much longer he expected to work and his answer was, "I have two doubles left to go." I really admire Brian for sticking to and remaining focused on his personal financial goals. Brian shared his past investment performance with me and I was a bit stunned. This really great teacher does a better job at managing his own money than many professional investment advisors in the business today. The points being that you don't have to be in the business to do a really good job of Managing Your Own Money!

Chapter 8

PORTFOLIO CONSTRUCTION EXPLAINED

Investment Objectives

Aggressive Growth

This objective is most suitable for someone under the age of 35. The mix is generally 100% stock mutual funds. Rarely is the Aggressive Investor interested in bonds or other asset classes. The portfolio is concentrated in faster growing mid cap funds, international, and specialty funds. The emphasis is on Growth over Value mutual funds.

Growth

This objective is most suitable for someone under the age of 60. The mix for a growth investor is 80% value, blend, and growth oriented stock funds and 20% in bond or real estate funds. Of the 80%, large cap and mid cap funds are favored with the emphasis on value-oriented funds as you near retirement.

Growth and Income

This objective is most suitable for someone over the age of 50. The mix for a growth and income investor is 60% stock funds and 40% in bond funds. This is also the mix for a **Balanced Account**. Value funds are a top choice for this objective. Small cap funds are rarely used with this objective. Already retired, a mix of 50% stocks and 50% bonds is okay too.

Once you have determined your investment objective of Growth, Conservative Growth, or Growth and Income, you are ready to construct your portfolio. I held to a strict minimum of **five mutual funds** and still do to this day. The reason you want to own five funds is to take full advantage of all the best performing funds within their respective investment styles of, Large Cap Growth, Large Cap Value, Mid Cap growth or value, foreign, bonds, metals, and real estate to name a few asset classes.

The S&P 500 has a Beta of 1. A Beta of 1 is the amount of movement up or down in the S&P 500. For example, a portfolio that has a beta of .6 takes 60% of the risk or movement of the S&P 500. A stock with a Beta of 1.5 can be expected to move or fluctuate 50% more than the S&P 500. A five-fund format almost (but not always) has a lower Beta than the S&P 500, which is categorized as growth and income. What you are looking for is the most amount of gain for the least amount of risk.

To demonstrate this to high school seniors taking my Personal Money Management classes, I draw five circles on the blackboard: one in the center and four around the larger middle circle. In the center circle is your Core Holding. Funds with a low Standard Deviation, perhaps a Value Fund are excellent candidates for a Core Holding. A top performing diversified Global fund investing around the world could also qualify for the top job of Core Holding. Depending on the amount of money you are allocating, you can use two funds in that center circle. In the outside circles go Large Cap, Mid Cap, Foreign, Real Estate, Bonds, Small Cap your choice.

My favorite mix of percentages for a five-fund format was 30, 25, 20, 15, and 10. The top three funds manage 75% of the money. I used the 15% and 10% circles to put smaller amounts of money to work in a single fund such as a Small Cap fund or Sector fund such as real estate. I asked the class, "How many funds do we want to own?" When they hold up five fingers, I know they have got it. Is it okay to just put 20% in five different funds? Yes, that is okay but I like to overweight certain funds to enhance performance. Do I really care about which funds you put in each of those percentages? No, because I know that Wall Street is picking funds for you off your Watch List. With that 14.4% requirement over the last five years, it is going to be really hard for you to invest in an under performing lonesome loser. If you get a slowpoke horse, hitch him up to the back of your financial wagon and sell him when you get to the next town.

Chapter 9

HOW ASSET ALLOCATION WORKS

Asset Allocation is the single largest determinant to a portfolio's performance at yearend. Different asset classes (stocks, bonds, real estate, metals, and cash) normally have non-correlated or different rates of returns each year. Portfolio Diversification reduces the overall financial risk in terms of the unpredictable and variability of returns year-over-year. Sixty percent of a portfolio's performance at year-end can be attributed to the **asset allocation** or the amount of money invested within each asset class. The actual mutual fund or ETF selection is said to produce twenty percent of a portfolio's performance. That same study found another twenty percent of a portfolio's performance at year-end can be attributed to current economic conditions.

Your specific asset allocation will be affected by your ability to accept risk and your time horizon. Those with a long time horizon before they need to use investment assets can afford to take higher risks. Someone using or about to use investment assets to provide current income needs to alter their allocation to reduce risk.

When in private practice, I felt the mutual fund selection process was easy. Assigning the amount of money to a specific fund was my single biggest decision. This is where I matched risk to the client's objective.

Mutual Fund Choices Within Each Objective

Aggressive Growth – 100% Stocks

30% Small or Mid Cap

25% Foreign, Small, or Mid Cap

20% Foreign, Large Cap, Mid Cap, Small Cap

15% Foreign, Sector Fund, Large Cap, Mid Cap, Small Cap

10% Emerging Markets, Foreign, Sector Fund, Large Cap, Mid Cap, Small Cap, Metals, Specialty

Personally, I have never cared much for Small Cap funds. The universe of funds is small and fund companies like to close them to new investors early on to keep the fund small. Volatility is usually caused by a lack of diversification. They do take a hit during stock market corrections. You have to like volatility to invest in small cap funds. I would pick two Mid Cap funds for my 30% core position. Foreign 25% is a top choice with maybe two funds and Large Cap for the 20% allocation in just one fund. I would select a REIT real estate investment trust for the 15% and 10% to a specialty fund, sector, or small cap fund.

Growth Account – 80% Stocks 20% Bonds

30% Large Cap, Mid Cap

25% Large Cap, Mid Cap, Foreign

20% Bonds, Large Cap, Mid Cap, Foreign

15% Bonds, Large Cap, Mid Cap, Small Cap, Foreign

10% Real Estate Fund, Bonds, Small Cap, Emerging Market Debt

Growth is my favorite objective. I prefer Mid Cap to Large Cap for the 30% core holding because Mid Cap companies are growing faster than Large Cap companies. You can temper risk by using one Mid Cap Growth and one Mid Cap Value fund. Two Foreign funds, perhaps one Large Cap and one European Emerging Market fund fit nicely in the 25% allocation. Twenty Percent invested in bonds works for me. In the 15%, I like specialty funds such as a Long/Short fund or Real Estate. Ten percent is the perfect allocation for funds with a higher standard deviation or funds with less than 30 holdings.

Growth and Income – 60% Stocks / 40% Bonds also referred to as **Balanced**

30% Large Cap, Foreign

25% Large Cap, Bonds, Foreign

20% Large Cap, Bonds, Mid Cap, Foreign

15% Large Cap, Bonds, Mid Cap, Foreign, Real Estate

10% Real Estate Fund, High Yield Bonds, Emerging Market Debt

Again, risk is adjusted for the conservative Growth and Income investor. To diversify away risk, I would use a conservative Value oriented Large Cap U.S. fund and diversified Foreign mutual fund for the 30% core holding. I would put 25% in individual bonds U.S. and 15% in High Yield bonds U.S. I like Mid Cap for the 20% using two funds for more diversification. If the client were retired, I would put the 10% in a Real Estate Investment Trust (REIT), ETF or mutual fund.

The above is only to illustrate the thought process by which I did my asset allocation for client accounts. Based on client objectives and risk tolerance, percentages and choices in Growth or Value funds could be different. Conservative investors may want to use more Value funds in building their portfolio. All investors need to know their risk tolerance and suitability for each specific investment. Investors need to take into consideration their age, income, net worth, time horizon, and need for liquidity before investing. Investment Advisors are taught to tell investors that they need to give their investments a minimum of three years to work before they need the money for other purposes. I see myself as an investor for life.

Help for the First Time investor

Investing on Wall Street can be intimidating. First time investors worry most about losing their money. Fear can make you feel like you are sitting on pins and needles. Who could possibly want to jump into a cold swimming pool on a cold day? Having an investment that goes up and down is like standing on a fault line waiting for an earthquake. It is fear of the unknown if you have never invested before. Human emotions get in the way of all investors from time to time. First time investors usually invest small amounts. Because it is all of their money, the risk of even a small loss can give them the willies. We all have a tendency to draw a line in the sand noting the amount of money invested. We tend to remember the highest our accounts reached and when. Generally we have only one horse pulling our financial wagon. All our money is riding in the saddlebags of just one horse. As long as there is profit in the account we are happy as can be. New investors hold onto their accounts until they start to lose money. We start to take a little heat and we lose a little more. Thinking they are going to lose it all, they run for the exit to post their loss. Investment losses are some of the best-kept secrets. We are quick to brag about our winnings yet reluctant to admit we ever made a financial mistake. All investors have lost money on more investments than they care to admit. My clients never did like to see their monthly statements fluctuate in value but increases and decreases in price is how we make our money. Wall Street bids prices up and down sometimes significantly in both directions.

When you think about it, everything we own goes up and down in value every single day. Cars lose some of their value every single day and we think nothing of it. Homes were increasing in value and now they are going down. Homes are where we live; investing in the growth of American enterprises on Wall Street is where we make our money!

Here are some things we can do to get over fear of fluctuation.

- Start out small so the fluctuations look small.

- Add to your investment every month. Buying more shares monthly, **Dollar Cost Averaging***, will lower your cost basis, which will help your account get into the black faster.

- Give your investment room to work. **Scalping** the market is buying and selling stocks on the same day. A **Swing Trade** can go on for a few days to a few weeks. A **Position Trade** is one that you expect to hold for a year or longer. **Make all your trades Position Trades**.

- Pick mutual funds with a low Standard Deviation of 10 or less. If that does not put you to sleep nothing will. I hate to admit it but I did use funds with a low Standard Deviation to put timid clients to sleep so I could go on about my work of making them money. Mutual funds Standard Deviation can be found on Morningstar.com. In the quote box, enter the symbol of your mutual fund. On the left, click on Risk Measures and there it is.

- Diversify away risk by working towards owning at least five mutual funds.

* **Dollar Cost Averaging** – This is a wonderful investment strategy especially for the beginning investor. By investing a fixed amount monthly or quarterly, more shares are purchased when the market is low and less when the market is high. The end result of investing at regular intervals is your average cost is less than the current price if the market is trading within a range.

There are two events that are big concerns for investor's accounts and those are during times of <u>War</u> and <u>Recession</u>. Even the expectation of such events drives stock prices down. Early warnings ahead of these events give you time to adjust your allocation to cash, or other asset classes.

How to Figure a Portfolio Rate of Return

Even computers struggle with calculating one rate of return for an entire portfolio. Money market accounts are crediting interest on idle cash. Mutual funds lower their share price when dividends and capital gains are credited to the account. Mutual funds are bought and sold during the year, which adds even more confusion for the best of computer programs.

Calculating a portfolios internal rate of return is not all that hard. I simply take last years closing account values on December 31, subtract the portfolios current value, and divided that number by the December 31 closing account value. If last years closing account value was $324,955.27 and the current value of the account is $354,259.77, simply subtract $324,955.27 from $354,259.77 to get $29,304.50. Divided the year-end total of $324,955.27 into $29,304.50 and you get 9.01%. How easy is that?

Chapter 10

TROUBLE WITH TECHNICAL ANALYSIS

Technical Analysis has been around for a very long time. Market technicians have wanted to find an indicator that will tell them when to buy and when to sell. Formulas are being written into software programs to help traders increase the accuracy of their trades.

Tactical Asset Allocation is an investment style that rebalances portfolios based on market conditions and not a calendar. Technical Analysis is used to adjust the amount of money invested in a given asset class that is expected to outperform in the near term, say three to six months. I use Standard Deviation and the Predictor as a guide to which funds might be candidates for sale during periods of market weakness. You don't need to sell everything to cushion market volatility.

Strategic Asset Allocation rebalances investments in a portfolio based on a calendar, usually quarterly but sometimes semiannually or annually. Strategic Asset Allocation stays fully invested throughout a market cycle and is considered a buy and hold strategy for three years or longer. I have never favored Strategic Asset Allocation alone because it rebalances money to under-performing asset classes. I would rather see money directed to asset classes that Wall Street likes best and are moving higher.

Technical Analysis tries to determine the trend or direction of the stocks and bonds by looking at past pricing of a stock or mutual fund. A market analyst is an expert who will know tomorrow why the things he predicted yesterday didn't happen today. Better than those market analysts are the technicians in the trade that use charts and graphs to show a change of trend from up to down and vise versa. All traders want to jump on a trend and make some money. Investment guru Marty Zweig was the first to coin the phrase, **"The Trend is your Friend"** and I agree. Screen traders look for trends on one and five minute intra-day charts. They are said to be Scalping the market when buying and selling the same day. For some reason they find it hard to hold a position overnight. They want a 100% cash position or are flat at the end of each days trading. Very few day-traders make money. In fact, most day-traders end up losing their shirts. Commodity Dealers know this and will often take the opposite side of their trades. Swing Traders are looking to hold a trade over a few days to a few weeks. Position Traders want to hold an investment a year or longer. As I said before, you have to give your investments time to work. Traders provide a lot of liquidity and volume to the marketplace and little else.

I am a Position Trader and am always thinking that I am going to own all my investments forever, which is not the case. By nature, I do not consider myself an active trader although when my Predictor speaks, I listen.

VDE
is range
bound
(for now)

Something Very Important to know!

The overall market and or individual stock is either **Range Bound** or **Trending** up or down. Range Bound simply means something is trading back and forth within a certain price range. Price oscillates within a price range. A stock for example might trade back and forth between $10 and $18 over the course of several months. When the market is going up at a steady pace or down at a steady pace it is said to be **trending**. A **two-line** moving average is the best technical indicator when the market is **Trending**. When the market is **Range Bound**, the Predictor works perfectly.

I spent more than a decade trying to come up with an indicator that was highly accurate. About the best I could find was a simple two-line moving average. One line averages **21 periods** of prices and another shorter line averages **9 periods** of price. A signal is created when the faster moving 9-period moving average crosses the longer but slower moving 21-period moving average.

All the charts in this book are courtesy of
Chip Anderson at Stockcharts.com

Here is a good example of a Range Bound Stock: The price ranges between $35 and $43 per share.

Chart A

Here is a good example of a stock that is trending.

Chart B

Apple shows us a trend in both directions.

Chart C

The two-line moving average is great for showing trend but the negative is that it makes a late call and produces a fair number of whipsaws leaving you **in** the market when you are supposed to be **out** or **out** when you are supposed to be **in**. In addition, a two-line moving average makes really late calls on weekly charts. It is best used on daily, hourly, or minute charts. I looked at Stochastic, Moving Average Convergence Divergence (MACD), the Relative Strength Indicator (RSI) and every other indicator known to man. At one time, I wrote my own indicator of indicators. The problem with all technical analysis is that it is **trend following**, which is like trying to drive your car by looking in the rear view mirror. Can you imagine driving your car by looking out your rear window at where you have been rather than out the front window, which is where you want to go?

I befriended a floor trader, turned screen trader, who threw them all in the trash except for one. My trashcan was full of indicators too. But don't despair; there is one indicator worth it's weight in gold. Please allow me to introduce you to the **Commodity Channel Index**. How I learned to use the CCI became **The Predictor**.

Chapter 11

THE MIGHTY COMMODITY CHANNEL INDEX

starts bottom prev pg

The Commodity Channel Index (CCI) as it is called, is the brainchild of Don Lambert. Thinking that commodities trade in a range up and down, Don came up with a dandy formula to show graphically a change in trend. The original default still is 20 periods of minutes, days, or weeks of pricing. But Ken Wood, founding father of Woodie's CCI Club, got it right using just 14 periods of price. To make sure 14 was the correct number; I experimented with periods ranging from 6 to 30. Fourteen dialed it in just perfectly!

I have come up with my own set of rules when it comes to reading the CCI indicator. The CCI is made up of a Zero Line, a + 100 line − 100 line, a plus 200 line, a minus 200 line, +-300 and so on. The chart turns green above 100 and magenta below 100, which we will see shortly. According to Don Lambert a buy signal occurs when the line crosses the +100 line into the green to enter a long trade and when crossing the −100 line for a short trade. **In my work**, you **buy** (get Long) when magenta ends with the cross of the −100 line to the upside. You sell some or all of your position when green ends with the crossing of the + 100 line to the downside. Long Positions are never entered when price (the gray line) is wandering aimlessly in-between the 100 lines. You can cover a position or sell in-between the 100 lines but that is it. **The most profitable trades happen at the extremes**. Like a finger pointing down, here is where you buy and a finger pointing up is where you sell. Many say you can't time the market but I disagree.

The Predictor is primarily based on <u>a Divergence</u>, the strongest signal of them all. A Divergence is where you draw an imaginary line from the bottom of the magenta to the bottom of the next magenta. If the line goes up between those two you have a Divergence IF price made a lower low between the two magentas. Draw an imaginary line under the price action between the two magentas. If price made a low and then went on to trade at a lower low, you have a Divergence. A divergence of the CCI and price is when you have one line headed in one direction and the other line headed in the other direction. Here is what it looks like:

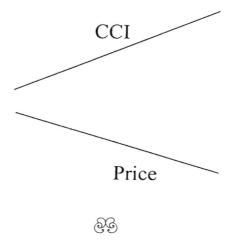

Chapter 12

THE PREDICTOR

Authors note

There are multiple examples of The Predictor in this chapter. Don't be discouraged after my analysis of the first chart. There are plenty more to follow including two for you to annotate at the end.

Chart E

The **Predictor** is a technology that tells the investor when to enter and exit their trades.

Traders are pretty much trend followers. They want to be long the stock on the way up and short the stock on the way down. For the most part, traders largely determine Price Action you see above. Buyers are said to be in control of a stock's price on the way up and sellers are in control of the stock's price on the way down.

Sell

The Predictor is a **Divergence** between the CCI and price action. At market tops, price will make a higher high and the CCI will show a lower high indicating that buying strength is ending. At market bottoms, prices will make a lower low and the CCI will make a higher low indicating that selling strength is ending.

Buy

In the chart E, price made a higher high on December 17 than it did on December 1. The CCI shows a lower high on December 13 than it did on November 28 indicating a change in the direction of price is coming and it is time to exit the position at or near $48.

On chart E, there are several other ways of using the CCI besides the highly accurate Divergence. One, you **never** enter a trade to buy between the +-100 and 0 line. Daily charts are for Swing Traders looking to only hold a trade for a few days to a week or two. For my purposes, I'll post my profit in order to re-enter the position at a lower price adding some additional mutual fund shares to my account. Best use of the Predictor is selling in the green at the cross of the +100 line and buying in magenta at the cross of the −100 line on the highly accurate **WEEKLY** Chart.

When price stops going higher and starts down, buyers return to drive the price back up to where it stopped. When that happens, price is said to have made a Double Top. When price stops going down and starts up, sellers return to drive the price back down to where it stopped. When that happens, price is said to have made a Double Bottom. Double Tops and Double Bottoms happen very regularly and they are also an indication of a change of direction. Add Double Tops and Double Bottoms to the Divergence and you have a very strong signal. You can see the Double Top on October 10 at $49.38 and on October 30 at $49.24.

Professional traders will scale into and out of their positions at these various buy and sell points and at Double Tops and Bottoms. Just remember the bread and butter trade **is the Divergence!**

On the next page I would like to show you how to determine the market's trend. You will make more money if you trade with the trend. It is also important to know when the trend is about to change. The chart on the next page will show you **market trend**.

To use the Predictor chart for market trend, you only have to change one setting at the bottom of the screen and that is from a Daily Chart to a Weekly Chart.

$SPX is the S&P 500 Index, which consists of 500 companies meeting Standard and Poor's criteria for mid and large cap U.S. companies.

Weekly Chart of the S&P 500

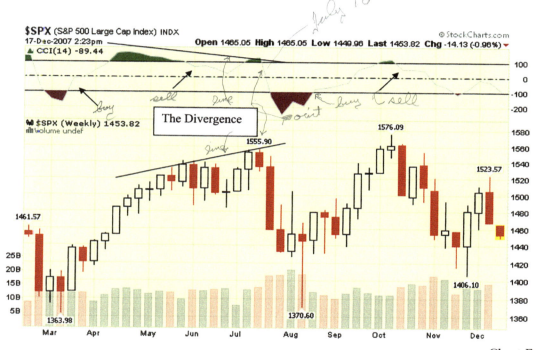

Chart F

This is a really great chart to talk about. Here you have a Weekly Chart of the S&P 500. Around March 10, you can see the magenta end with the cross of the - 100 line producing a buy signal. There is a sell in the last week of May with the green end with a cross of the +100 line.

Then came the Divergence on July 10 with a lower low in the green and a higher high in weekly price. What did the S&P do? It went down hard. The next buy signal occurred in the middle of August at the cross of the - 100 line up. What did price do? It went up. **The longer your timeframe, weekly in this case, the more accurate the chart is**. What we have next is a Double Top and a sell in the first week of October with a cross of the +100 line.

Here is what happened after December 20, 2007.

Chart G

The next buy signal occurred during the first week of February with a cross of the magenta −100 line at around 1350. Then came the Divergence on March 17 as all the sellers ran out of gas.

Price made a lower low at 1256.98 on March 17 and the CCI made a higher low at 101.66. I sent an email to my teacher friends telling them about the signal. I bought a mutual fund that has climbed 18% higher and a stock that is 35% higher. We are in the sell zone but there is no signal yet. I am not a believer in market timing. That is to say sell 100% of everything with every signal. I think that is crazy. You miss some of the downside when you raise cash but you also miss some of the upside when you do that. Investors using Technical Analysis to cushion a down market fare better than those who use Strategic Asset Allocation or buy and hold. In an up market, Strategic Asset Allocation investors make more money because they have been fully invested from the market low.

In my practice, I would only sell those funds with a high standard deviation. In a five-fund format, two to three might be sold. The other reason I did that was to find a better performing mutual fund portfolio to own when the market turned back up. That is exactly what I did on March 18. I replaced the fund I sold in the fall with a new fund picked by my 4-week Mid Cap moving average. That fund is still number one on the 4-week and should remain so for the balance of the year.

Now lets see what the Predictor has to say about a mutual fund:

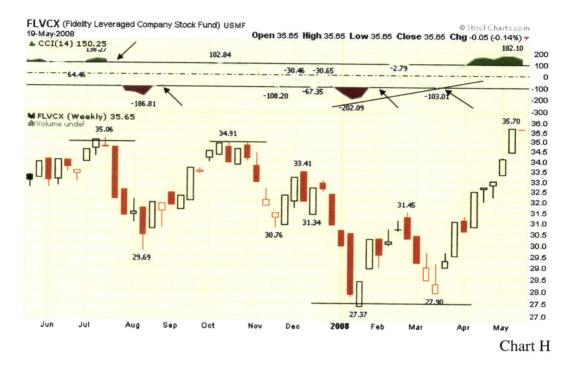

Chart H

The fund starts out in the **sell zone** oh, darn! We wait. We get our buying opportunity on August 10 with a cross out of magenta at the −100 line. Let's pretend we missed the Double Top on October 10 so we stayed long the fund at $31 per share.

Our next buy opportunity on chart H came at the cross out of magenta on January 25 or so at $30 and you decide to add to your position. What does the market do? It goes down. Then the fund decided to make a Double Bottom at 27.90 on March 15. You look at the CCI and see your **bread and butter** Divergence strong buy signal and you rub your hands together and add to your position at $29. So what happened after that? Hopefully by now you are beginning to see what I see on the CCI. By the way, the length of the candle is the highest and lowest price during that week of trading. That last week of trading prices ranged from $33.90ish to $35.70. Using the Weekly, you stay long for weeks on end. Most funds companies impose a 2%

early redemption fee to sell within 60 days of purchase. Another reason to have a five-fund format. There is always a fund that is past the 60-day early redemption fee.

The Bullish Percent Index

Let's take a look at **the Bullish Percent Index**, a market breadth indicator. The index is calculated by dividing the number of stocks on the New York Stock Exchange that are currently trading with Point and Figure buy signals by the total number of stocks on the exchange. I have always liked the Bullish Percent Index because it tells me how healthy the market is at the moment. I also use it as a confirmation. For example, when I saw the Predictor fire off a strong buy signal March 17, the Bullish Percent Index confirmed it. The CCI is not used with the Bullish Percent Index because it does not generate a buy or sell signal.

Chart I

The line chart prints red when the trend is down and black when the trend is up. Just with your eye, you can clearly see the trend changed after March 17. Can you see the Double Bottom on March 10th, and again on March 17? This was just another signal that the market was about to turn up.

So right now that index on chart I is saying that the market is pretty healthy at the moment with 63.2% of the stocks in Point and Figure buy signals. I looked at the line coming down pointing right at March 17 when it said to me, "If you are going to get long, this would be the ideal place to do it."

Would the Predictor have worked back in 2005?

Chart J

Here is a look at IBM price action beginning on September 20, 2005. This is the Predictor at work on a Daily chart. It also works on a 5-minute chart if you are trading intra-day. It looks like a buy down there in the magenta with a signal on September 27 with a cross of the −100 line. So, we get long. The sell signal to get out of IBM comes on October 18 with a cross of the +100 line. So, what did price action do after that? You are right if you said it went down. By the way, do you see the Divergence in October? You should be seeing those by now. So now we are sitting on the sidelines feeling all kinds of happy and smart like a fox.

So let's see when we can get long here in 2005. Oh wait; there is another little mini Divergence around November 1 on chart J. Selling looks like it is running out of gas so I'm going to buy here. This is going to be a really nice trade!! When do we get out of this trade? Well, the Predictor says I should close the position on November 29th with the cross of the +100 line. The Predictor has us long the market on the way up and showed us where to sell back in 1995. In 1995, I was just starting to learn about moving averages. Technical Analysis was still in the distant future for the average trader.

Sometimes its best to just be long the market and forget trading it. The next two charts K and L are from 2003.

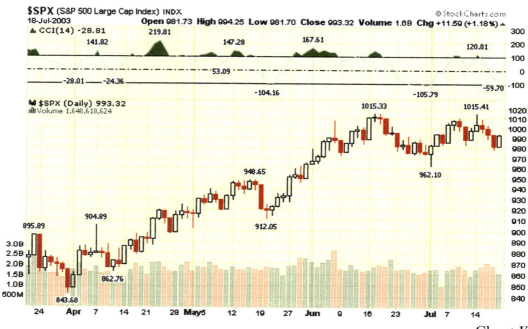

Chart K

Chart L

Taking a Look at the Big Picture

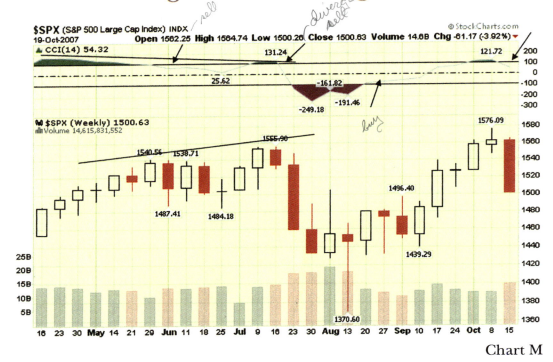

Chart M

If you find yourself struggling with a daily chart, create a weekly chart (Charts M and N). The sell signal here is on June 1, 2007. The Divergence catches your eye on July 20. The buy is on August 20 with another sell on October 15 and then watch what happens after October 18.

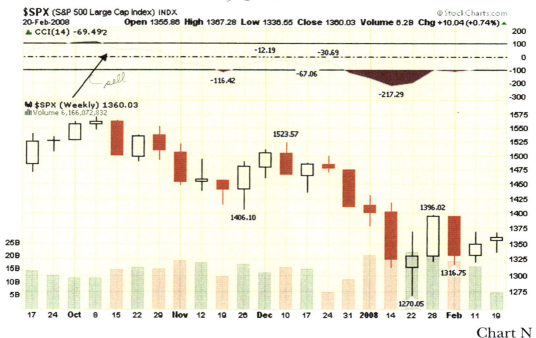

Chart N

A Chart That Produces Less Trades

Chart O

I prefer charts that produce fewer trades as Chart O shows. If you watch things too closely, **managing your own money** can make you a nervous wreck. For busy people on the go, the big picture keeps you long through the ups and downs of daily economic numbers. The above chart shows a sell signal during the last week of December followed by a buy signal on March 1st. That is two trades in 6-months. What has me worried in chart O is that the chart ends in the sell zone. A sell signal is in the works. A cross of that +100 line and I must bring something to cash.

If this is all new to you I suggest you paper trade until you gain enough confidence to use real money. Just a yellow note pad and pencil is all you need to get started. Write down the date, symbol, name of the investment, the price per share and the amount of money you would have invested.

Make a list of mutual funds, stock, or Exchange Traded Funds (ETFs) because you are going to be looking for range bound candidates. The market can trend in a steady line up as well as Trend in a steady line down. What you will be looking for are candidates that trade within a price range. If you are looking at slow and steady returns over time, mutual funds make the most sense and you should not have to trade them all that often.

Another Power Packed Indicator with Punch

There is one other indicator that can be used with The Predictor and that is the McClellan Summation Index. Developed by Sherman and Marian McClellan, the McClellan Oscillator is a breadth indicator derived from each day's net advances, the number of advancing issues less the number of declining issues.

The Summation Index is simply a longer-range version of the McClellan Oscillator. Whereas the McClellan Oscillator is used for short to intermediate trading purposes, the Summation Index provides a longer-range view of market breadth and is used to spot major market turning points, as does The Predictor. Used together on a Daily Chart, they make a nice combination. The Symbol for the New York Stock Exchange (NYSE) Summation Index is $NYSI.

Once you have The Predictor up and running just enter the Symbol $NYSI and press Enter. Scroll down to Indicators on the left and Select Price and to the right of that select Behind Price and press Update.

The Summation Index works best on a Daily Chart. You can use it in one of two ways. One, you can used it to trade the S&P 500. Two, you can use it to time other funds that go up and down with the rest of the market.

Chart P

The smooth line is the Summation Index. The jagged line is the S&P 500. The Summation Index line turns red to indicate a change in trend to down. A change in color to black shows a change in trend to up. You can see that it lines up quite nicely with The Predictor. The signal is strong when you have two Indicators in sync.

From the left, you can see the Sell Signal on February 28. The Buy Signal is on March 22. There is a short whipsaw on April 14 but then turned black again and stays black all the way to May 20.

Are you ready to try your hand at The Predictor? Take a look at chart Q and R to see if you can figure out when to buy and when to sell.

Now try your hand at the Predictor

see next pg

Chart Q

Tell me if you can see the Divergences on this chart?

Chart R

The first chance to get long is on March 11 with the cross of the −100 line at $37 a share. When did you decide to sell? It would have been March 27 for me with the cross of the +100 line at $43 a share. The next buying opportunity comes on April 15 at $42.50 per share. A nice earnings report at the end of April drives the price up to $53.40. The sell comes on May 7 at $51.50. It looks like it is ready to fire off another buy signal on May 28.

If you got most of that right, you own the Predictor. Just remember the Predictor works best when the market, stock, or mutual fund is Ranging. When the market is Trending, we get long on a pull back.

Where are you placing your buys and sells?

Where is the first Divergence? Where is the second Divergence? On March 18, Goldman Sacks gapped up on a Divergence so you might have gotten long at 165. Selling ended with a whimper on March 14. Do you see the Double Bottom on March 28 and on April 15? That little bit of Magenta tells me that sellers ran out of gas and the Double Bottom are both signs of a change of direction. You could still be long from March 18 and down $4 a share. Sometimes you just have to stay long in the trade and wait. The sell is an easy one on the Divergence on May 5 with the cross of the +100 line at about $195.50. That is a $3,000 profit in 7 weeks!

Turning you into a trader is not the purpose of sharing the Predictor with you. I just want you to have a piece of technology that can guide you as to when to buy and when to sell. I still prefer you use the Predictor on a Weekly chart in order to keep your trading to a minimum. The Predictors purpose is to help you adjust your asset allocation in times of market weakness. The above was an example of a Swing Trade.

It is human nature to make up excuses not to act or believe in signals generated by technical indicators. To dispel disbelief, I suggest paper trading using buy and sell signals until you are convinced of their accuracy and are comfortable using them. Investors will gain more confidence paper trading today's market than paper trading past performance. There is no doubt in my mind that The Predictor and the McClellan Summation Index will exceed your expectations.

Creating The Predictor

Go to: www.Stockcharts.com

1. Select **Free Charts**
2. Enter the **symbol** $spx for the S&P 500 ← @ top of pg
3. Scroll down to enter the **settings below**.

Chart Attributes

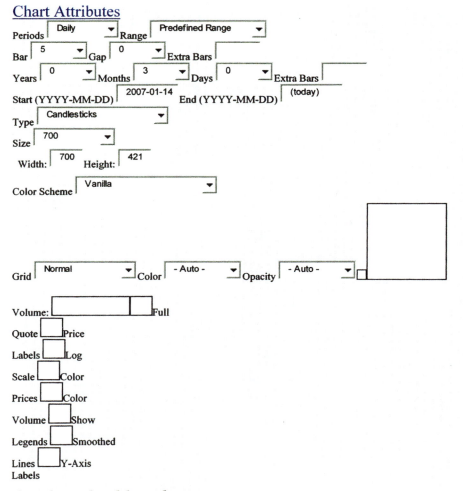

Periods: Daily ▼ | Range: Predefined Range ▼

Bar: 5 ▼ | Gap: 0 ▼ | Extra Bars:

Years: 0 ▼ | Months: 3 ▼ | Days: 0 ▼ | Extra Bars:

Start (YYYY-MM-DD): 2007-01-14 | End (YYYY-MM-DD): (today)

Type: Candlesticks ▼

Size: 700 ▼

Width: 700 | Height: 421

Color Scheme: Vanilla ▼

Grid: Normal ▼ | Color: - Auto - ▼ | Opacity: - Auto - ▼

Volume: _____|Full

Quote |__| Price

Labels |__| Log

Scale |__| Color

Prices |__| Color

Volume |__| Show

Legends |__| Smoothed

Lines |__| Y-Axis
Labels

Overlays should read **none**.

Indicators should read **CCI** Parameter **14** Position **Above**

Chapter 13

BONDING WITH BONDS

Gaining an Interest in Bonds

Bonds are an investment class and very unique. Investors and financial advisors often overlook investing in bonds. Loaning money to Americas most credit worthy borrowers is less risky than investing in shares of common stocks. It adds stability to investment portfolios. Bonds provide income to fund budgets for retirees. Bonds help you sleep at night because they keep a river of revenue coming in your financial door. Americans ongoing love affair with bonds is huge. Governments state and local and corporations require access to capital. The bond market is 25.2 trillion and still growing.

Almost one billion dollars in bonds are traded every business day. Who buys bonds? Institutions made up of pension plans, insurance companies, and mutual funds top the list. Governments and investors worldwide share a vested interest in our US debt obligations. Individual bond investors such as you and I own 10% of all outstanding debt. Baby Boomers are just beginning to buy bonds by the bushel.

Bonds – are easier to buy than ever. Not only are bonds traded on exchanges but also some are listed and sold through **The Bond Desk.** You can invest in bond mutual funds but I prefer owning individual bonds. To keep their distribution competitive, mutual funds often pay out all the interest plus a little bit of principal causing a decline in Net Asset Value over time. Interest rate risk causes Net Asset Values to fluctuate as rates rise and fall.

If the direction of interest rates is down, the Net Asset Value goes up. In times of rising interest rates, Net Asset Values go down. Maturities within a mutual fund can extend as far as 30 years. The portfolio average is a lot less than that but still carry a lot of interest rate risk. I'm not looking for a fluctuation in Net Asset Value. I am interested income and all of my money back upon maturity.

I prefer owning bonds directly through Zions Direct, who specializes in "bonds for less." They give you access to all the bonds on the Bond Desk and only charge a $10.95 commission on each trade. Normally the markup on bonds is a point and a half to three points. A point and a half is $15 per $1,000 bond. Invest $25,000; a full service broker will hide $375 in commissions in the price of the bond. You could pay up to three points or $30 per bond times 25 bonds and you will be paying $750. That $10.95 is a whole lot less, which yields more to the investor and if you don't mind my saying, Zions offers excellent service.

Wall Street brokerage firms take care of themselves first. Even $375 is not good enough for some brokerage firms. They often package bonds and slap the investor with a 3% commission based on the amount invested. Yikes! It is better that you do it yourself over at Zions Direct (http://www.zionsbank.com/zd_index.jsp). Zions Direct can help you set up a screen to find the bonds that meet your personal investment objective. For example if you only wish to invest in FDIC Insured Certificates of Deposit's (CD) a screen can be set up to search for CD offerings from banks all around the country at the push of a computer key.

CD's in the secondary market have a much higher yield than if you walk into your local bank branch to purchase one. You can easily search and find attractive yields from Municipal Bonds, Agency bonds, and Corporate Bonds. Interestingly, small amounts of $5,000 or less generally have a higher yield than larger amounts giving the small investor an edge.

Searching for Bonds Made Easy

On the Bonds For Less page click on **ALL TAXABLE**. To search for all bonds coming due in 90-days, type a date 90-days from today in the **Maturity To** box. If you are looking for a specific yield enter it in the **Yield From** box. You can further define your search by selecting a range of Standard and Poor's ratings, coupon, price, and quantity of bonds for sale. It is easy to Include or exclude bonds that are callable and the number of bonds displayed on a single page. Because I want to see all the bonds, I enter 500 in the **Bonds**

Per Page box. At the bottom of the page select **Saved Queries** and type in 90-days, left click on **Save**, and you have just set up a search for all taxable bonds coming due over the next 90-days.

My favorite three searches are 90-day, 6-months, and 1-year. For a High Yield search for bonds coming due in 6-months, enter a date six months hence in the **Maturity To** box. In the **Yield From** box enter 6.5%. In the **S&P Rating** box **Minimum** Enter B+ to search for all bonds yielding 6.5% or better that are rated B+ or better over the next six months. To save this screen select **Save** and type in High Yield to 6-months so the next time you visit the Bond Desk all you have to do is select your Saved Query to display your criteria. Press the Search button and all the bonds for sale over the next six months meeting these criteria will be displayed at the push of a button.

To search for bonds maturing in 1-year, enter a date one year from today in the **Maturity To** box. In the **Yield From** box enter 5.5%. In the **S&P Rating Minimum** box enter BB+. Select **Save** and you are done. You have just made a predefined screen to search for all taxable bonds yielding 5.5% or better with a S&P rating of BB+ or higher coming due within the next 12-months. The Bond Desk has made your search for bonds quick and easy.

Bonds prices do fluctuate daily. The longer the duration before the bond matures; the more sensitive they are to changes in interest rates. As bonds get closer to maturing, their prices slowly creep back to par or $1,000 per bond. I personally won't go out longer than 4 years and prefer shorter maturities especially in a rising interest rate environment. There is always an ample supply of bonds maturing in the next 12 months, which helps to minimize fluctuations in price. Locking rates up by extending maturities is something you want to do if interest rates are falling, but not too far. Bonds are best held to maturity, as bond investors are interested in the interest and their money back at maturity. Bond interest is reported on a 1099-tax form and capital gains come to you on your December statement.

Bond ratings change based on economic conditions, the underlying issuer's financial condition, and their ability to pay. Bonds rated BBB and higher by Standard and Poor's are considered investment grade which "indicates an adequate capacity to pay interest and repay principal."

Do Bond Ratings Really Matter

A recent research report marks the first historical study of corporate bond defaults, covering the years 1990 through 2000. From Jan. 1, 1990 through Dec. 31, 2000, 49 Fitch-rated issuers defaulted on their long-term debt, out of a total of 2,639 issuers carrying a Fitch rating over the 11-year period. The average annual default rate for all rated global corporate obligors was 0.43%. For investment-grade issuers, the average annual default rate was 0.05%, compared with 2.95% for high yield, or speculative-grade, issuers. Another way of stating that number is to say is that 97.05% of high yield bonds paid interest during the holding period and principle at maturity. Even though the chances of default are small, 48 issuers defaulted on their debt. Does that mean all 48 issuers resulted in a total loss to investors? I think not. In corporate hierarchy, debts of the corporation are paid before common shareholder in the event of liquidation. Using techniques discussed in this chapter will minimize these risks. Should we base all our bond decisions on bond ratings? No. Do they have an affect on the price of the bond? Yes, and it is substantial. Move a bonds rating and price and yield will follow. This is just one more reason to keep your maturities short. Just for fun, take a look at the number of bonds rated B- and their yield to maturity. You will see many that appear to have ratings much higher than what is currently assigned to the bond. Are Standard and Poor's always jolly on the spot with their rating changes? No. The rating services scrambled to change corporate ratings in March 2008 when Gross Domestic Product (GDP) already had slowed to 1%. They were a day late and a dollar short as they say. Do they often overlook a company's rating? Yes.

Besides bond ratings by Moodys, Fitch, and Standard and Poor's, are there any other ways to determine risk when looking at a bond? Yes, there is. The easiest is to look at the **yield to maturity**, which takes into account the bond coupon and the price per bond. Is the yield to maturity higher than the coupon or less than the coupon? If the yield to maturity is higher than the coupon, Wall Street bond investors have lowered the rating by lowering the price below par or $1,000 per bond. On the other hand if Wall Street bond investors are pricing the yield to maturity at less than the coupon then it can be inferred that the bond should be rated hither today than when the bond was first issued. In this example, the bond investor will be paying a premium over par or $1,000 lowering the yield to maturity below that of the coupon. Yield to maturity compared to the coupon is another method to determine a bonds true rating.

Buying the Best Bonds

There are more varieties of bonds than you can possibly imagine. A good-sized warehouse couldn't hold them all. The bond world has attached some pretty fancy names to them too like Inverse Floaters. There are bonds tied to the future price of a stock. If the price of the stock falls more than 20% then the value of your bond is converted into shares of the underlying stock. Wall Street firms lay awake at night dreaming of ways to fiddle around with bonds.

My recommendation is to say with tried and true. Only invest in bonds you are comfortable with. You don't have to take big risks to make a good steady income from bonds. I'll say it again; bond investors are largely interested in yield and the return of their money at maturity.

For guarantees, there are three bond investments that will work perfectly. I would first look at CD's for sale on the Bond Desk from banks all over the US. All are insured up to $100,000 per registration, how it is titled, per bank. You could have a bond registered in joint title, one individually, another held in joint title with a son or daughter. Many Municipal Bonds are insured giving them a AAA rating. Lastly, a 90-day or 6-month Treasury Bill is guaranteed by the US. These government guarantees are not free. Expect these bonds to yield less to the investor than their corporate cousins.

Investment grade corporate bonds rated BBB- by Fitch and Standard and Poor's and higher will give the bond investor a much higher rate of return. It is easy to pick almost any maturity you want. You can even pick bonds that pay monthly or semi-annual interest. I am completely comfortable with corporate bonds maturing in 90 days, 180 days, 9-months or a year and three months if that is what you want.

High yield bonds fluctuate too much in price to extend maturities much beyond two years. I try to keep my B+ and BB- rated bond maturities to less than one year preferably 3 to 6 months.

I do like revenue bonds. Municipalities raise money for projects that charge user fees. Roads and bridges that charge a toll provide revenues to pay timely interest and principal. Some bonds indentures set up rules requiring a sinking fund that is used to pay bond interest and principal at maturity. I am completely comfortable with all of these types of Municipal bonds. Insured Municipal bonds pay less interest but give a lot of comfort to conservative investors.

Building a Bond Ladder

Laddering bonds is easy to do. Buy one CD coming due in 90 days. Buy a second CD coming due in 6-months. Buy a third CD coming due in one year. The 90- day CD is your liquidity because it comes due every 90 days giving you access to cash in the event of emergency. Every 6-months you have a CD coming due and every year you have a CD coming due. Every 90 days different amounts are available for reinvestment. If interest rates are rising, laddering allows the bond investor to take advantage of higher rates every 90 days. Bond investors will extend maturities if interest rates are rising. The sweat spot in the yield curve might be 10 years to earn the best yield but four is my absolute maximum under any circumstances. Are you ready for a little surprise? You can use this same laddering technique with Corporate Bonds. It is very easy to get good quality corporate paper and ladder the maturities helping the investor earn a higher rate of return while maintaining short-term liquidity.

There are two ways to buy bonds in the open market; one is at the initial public offering and the other is in the open market. Bond Underwriters and the issuer set the coupon (interest rate) and the price per bond usually $1,000. Once the bond begins to trade, Wall Street bond investors set the price in the open market. I would much rather buy bonds in the open market than at the initial public offering price because I get to pick the company and the maturity often at a better price giving me a higher yield to maturity.

Fanning the Flames of Fear

As you and I both know commissionable broker dealers make their living instilling fear of further loss to motivate their customers to sell even their bonds. Unnecessary selling creates opportunities for seasoned bond investors. Some of the biggest profits can come to investors taking an opposite view of doom and gloom. Recently some small investor with $10,000 in bank bonds was coaxed into selling three months before expiration at a fairly substantial loss. I took the other side of that trade for a 16% yield to maturity. It is always wise to have cash on hand in order to take full advantage of these kinds of investment opportunities in both bond and stock markets. You can usually spot these kinds of opportunities because of the amount bonds for sale is usually small. Broker dealers are guilty of fanning the flames of fear to drive prices down and then turn about face.

JPMorgan hikes bonds from GM to 'buy'…. from Auto Insider July 23, 2008

> **JPMorgan Chase & Co.** raised its recommendation on the bonds of **General Motors Corp.** to "buy" from "sell," saying they have become cheap relative to rivals and the rest of the market. "Due to its considerable liquidity options as well as its vastly improved products, we believe GM is a sustainable entity," New York-based analysts Eric J. Selle and Atiba T. Edwards wrote in a report Tuesday. "We see more upside potential than downside risk at current levels."

How can broker dealers give good advise to their customers to Sell on one day and then give good advice to Buy on the next? Savvy investors and institutions knew GM had 27 billion dollars in their corporate treasury at the end of the first quarter 2008 while Broker Dealers were advising their customers to sell their GM bonds. I do have to complement JP Morgan for at least getting their customers on the other side of the trade. **As risk increases though, maturities must be shortened to 6-months or less.**

Determining the Direction of Interest Rates is not all that hard on Stockcharts.com. US Government Treasury yields show the direction of interest rates. The symbol for the 5-year US Treasury yield is $UST5Y. The yield on the 5-year Treasury is less than the yield on the 10- year Treasury $UST10Y. On either chart, the direction of interest rates is easily discernable. To determine the direction of short-term interest rates, take a look at the 2-year treasury $UST2Y. For a look at the ever popular 90-day Treasury Bill enter $UST3M. If interest rates are rising, bond investors will keep maturities short. If interest rates are falling, investors extend their maturities. Owning bonds until they mature out of the portfolio is the goal of every bond investor. For bond investors with plenty of patients, maturities longer than 4 years will seem like an eternity. A short ladder will still keep good yields well within reach. If you asked me to assign a percentage of bonds coming due in each year of a four-year holding period, it would look like this: 40% coming due in one year, 30% coming due in two years, 20% coming due in three years, and 10% coming due in four years.

Just as individuals seek to pay down their debt, institutions want to reserve the right to redeem or call in a certain dollar amount at various intervals. Issuers paying a premium above par to call in a bond is good reason to reinvest those profits somewhere else. Take their money and run, I say.

Managing Your Risks

As a Certified Financial Planner, I liked talking about risks with clients. Most financial advisors think a discussion about risk will kill the deal and end the discussion. That is totally untrue. Everyone should want to know precisely the amount risk they are taking. To sleep at night, investors need to know the risks they are taking.

Diversification is a good manager of risk. If you have 500 chickens and lose one chicken it is no big deal. There is a lot of safety in numbers. I will be the first to compliment anyone who shows me a well-diversified portfolio. To take full advantage of different investment styles, you already know that I insist on a minimum of five mutual funds in a portfolio. Five funds give me a beta of about .20 or 20% of the risk of the S&P 500. Lets have a big round of applause for diversifying our portfolios?

Limiting the amount of money invested is yet another way of controlling risk. Savvy investors keep their losses small. I always set limits to the amount of money clients were allowed to invest in a single issue. For example, I will buy a bond rated B+ but I will limit my investment to as little as $5,000 depending on the company and industry. In addition, a rating of B+ is as low as I will go when investing in bonds.

Asset Allocation or controlling an amount of money invested in any single asset class is another risk management technique. For example, real estate is an asset class so limiting the amount of money to that asset class is a good example of an investor using Asset Allocation to manage risk.

Based on Taxes, Where are the Best Places to Hold your Investments?

Bonds – Bonds carry less risk and are best held in a brokerage account outside of a tax-qualified plan. I like to put risk where it belongs inside a tax-qualified account because growth there is tax deferred, which is what you want. Bond interest is taxed as ordinary income and so are distributions from tax-qualified plans. For that reason, I have no problem with bonds being held in a tax-qualified plan but prefer mutual funds because of their taxable distributions at year-end.

Mutual Funds – The best places to invest in mutual funds is in qualified plans like IRA, 401K, 403b, defined benefit and profit sharing plans. Let the government share in some of the risk and reward. Mutual funds held in a brokerage account or at the fund report taxable capital gains and losses along with dividend distributions at year-end to you on 1099-tax form no matter how long you have held the shares. Mutual funds held outside of a tax-qualified account are best purchased after the fund trades X dividend and capital gains. Call the fund company to ask when their fund will trade X dividend and capital gains so you can avoid these increases in cost basis.

Stocks that are frequently traded or sold within one year are best held in an Individual Retirement Account (IRA) where withdrawals are taxed as ordinary income. Positions held for very long periods of time, a year or longer, can be held in a regular brokerage account and when sold taxed at lower Capital Gain rates.

A Short Conversation on Taxes

Taxes are harder to manage today then they were when tax brackets exceeded 70%. Prior to Ronald Reagan, for some Uncle Sam wanted 70 cents of every dollar earned. High tax rates discourage hard work. Why take a second job if the government is going to talk it all away? It discourages the American entrepreneurial spirit. High tax rates are anti-capitalism. To increase unemployment all you need to do is raise taxes on the entrepreneurs that hire employees. Bad tax policy limits growth and slows new technologies that we will need to compete in the new world economy. Sadly, there is very little we can do today to lower taxes.

Congress came up with the Alternative Minimum Tax (AMT) to limit the impact of tax shelters and deductions for higher income taxpayers. The AMT is nothing more than a second way of calculating the amount of taxes due, which has been a big bonanza for the US treasury. The government set the bar low enough that millions of taxpayers every year fall victim to the Alternative Minimum Tax for the first time. The only solution is to **simplify our tax code**.

Ways to Save Taxes

There are four basic ways to chip away at taxes. Money can qualify to be tax deductible, tax deferred, tax free, or provide tax credits.

You can exclude income from taxes by participating in a company pension plan. Individual Retirement Accounts allow individuals without a company pension to set aside money for retirement and receive a tax deduction for doing so.

Annuities offered by insurance companies are tax deferred. Growth in capital assets such as common stock and real estate are good examples of things we can own that are tax deferred. The Roth IRA is tax deferred and then comes out tax-free at retirement. Nice!

Getting involved in things that are tax-free sound most appealing. Interest from some Municipal Bonds is still tax-free but some aren't. Private Purpose Municipal Bonds that build sports stadiums or airport ramps for airline use are taxable. Enlarging a water district is an example of a Public Purpose Municipal Bond that would pay tax-free income to the bondholder.

The tax dodges I dislike most involve investments that need a tax break in order to make it attractive to investors. An example of this is investing in low income housing partnerships. Tax Credits are direct dollar-for-dollar deductions from your taxes. If you owe $18,000 in taxes and have a $2,000 tax credit then you own Uncle Sam only $16,000.

I never felt it was in the best interest of my clients to invest in something just because it came wrapped in tax-advantaged paper. Almost always there was nothing of value inside the box worth talking about. Just remember that no tax advantage can ever make up for a poor performing or really bad investment. Because our tax brackets are so low today, starting at 10%, taxes that use to dominate conversations with financial planners are exceedingly rare.

Chapter 14

RACING TOWARD RETIREMENT

Sadly, only 18 people out of 100 at age 65 are able to retire and live off their pension and Social Security benefits. **Of the 18, two will be <u>financially independent</u>.** Sixteen per one hundred will not live to age 65. Sixty-six people will continue to work, live with their children or be supported by their children, room with friends, or be supported by welfare or other social programs.

When the daily grind ends, retirement begins. We work most of all our lives for the opportunity to do what we want to do. Financial independence allows the retiree to focus on life's pleasures of travel, engage in hobbies, and be active within the community. Retirement for the baby boomer is not about bingo and ice cream socials. Baby boomers like my good friend Bill Porter has a big budget for bait. Bill finds his fun fishing off the Florida Keys in his Blue Bayou. Only economic freedom will allow us baby boomers to find their fun sailing blue waters or flying blue skies. If I'm not flying in my Cessna 172, I'm thinking about going flying. My head is in the clouds most, if not all, the time. I rode my airport bicycle over to my good friend Gary Houston's hanger today. He just couldn't wait to show me his new Garmin Transponder that squawks a number and altitude on an aircraft controller's radar. Anxious to try it out, we hopped in his beautiful Lark Commander and disappeared for two hours. Our fellow Musketeer Salvador Corona is always reminding us that "we are all 62-year teenagers."

How much money will you need to retire? That is very easy to figure, so get your calculator out. When we are working our income funds our monthly budget. Retirement income from all sources needs to be large enough to fund our budget when income from our employment ends. So let's say we have a monthly budget of $4,500 or $54,000 annually of which 20% is taxes. Divide $54,000 by .065 to find out that you will need $830,769.23. This amount will need to earn a portfolio rate of return of 6.5% interest to yield $54,000 each year to cover an annual budget. If plenty of golf is your game, make sure you have that covered in your retirement budget as well.

If you want to impress your friends and family ask them what their monthly budget is. Multiply the number times 12 to get the annual budget. Divide the number by an interest factor of .065 and press equal. That is all there is to find how much you'll need for retirement. You can of course subtract any fixed pensions or Social Security before making the calculation. For example, if your Social Insecurity statement says you can expect to collect $1,600 a month at 62 then a calculation would go like this. Annual budget, minus annual Social Security, divided by .065 to get to the additional amount needed to fund your budget. So, how do you know when you can retire? **You can retire when all your income sources are equal to your budget.**

Now you know why doing a budget is so doggone important. Budgets and Retirement go hand-in-hand. Other items to include in your retirement budget are reserves to purchase big-ticket items like your next car. Be sure and include a generous amount for travel, hobbies, and all the fun things you plan to do.

Last but not least, leave plenty of room in your budget for medical care because if you don't wear glasses now, you soon will. Get as many crowns installed while you have dental insurance to pay for it. Why do I use a conservative 6.5% distribution rate? I want some room for years in which your portfolio returns are less than 6.5%. If your returns are greater than 6.5% then you will have room in your budget to cover increases in the cost of living. If you wanted to be really conservative, use 5.5%.

I never advised clients to use distribution rates higher than 7%. Retirement is all about accumulating enough money to pay for the things we need. If the distributions rate is too high we face the danger of running out of money before we run out of birthdays. Some of my retired clients were asking for their investment accounts to earn double digit rates of return to fund their budget. I sent them letter after letter, year after year, informing them when they would run out of money to fund their budget. One of my clients started retirement with a million dollars. His budget was about $125,000 a year, which translates into a distribution rate of 12.5%! I could never get him to adjust that down. He ended up going back to work at age 72. The Social Security Administration is quick to point out that Social Security pays for 40% of retiree's budgets. You will have to come up with the rest.

Does our Asset Allocation change after we are retired? I say yes. If you are a growth investor before you retire, I think you should become more conservative in your retirement. I like balanced accounts best with 40% to 50% invested in yield from fixed interest investments such as bonds and real estate investment trusts and 50% to 60% invested in growth mutual funds.

It was rare to find a client with half their money in the market and the other half in bonds. Unless you are a widow, financial advisors are reluctant to talk about bonds because money stays in bonds for long periods without generating a new commission. The problem with having too much money in a tax-qualified account is that it gives you few choices when it comes to tax planning. You could live off principal for short periods in order to defer taxes into the next year if your capital is positioned properly. Plus, when you pay cash for a new car, taxes are added to the price of the car. A withdrawal of about 130% is needed to pay for the car and the taxes on the money that purchased the car.

Do I prefer the traditional IRA or do I prefer the Roth IRA? I am so glad you asked. I prefer the Roth IRA because tax savings from traditional IRAs end up being spent. For a person in a 25% tax bracket, a $3,000 traditional IRA contribution means your tax refund, assuming you get one, will increase by $750. It vanishes into thin air never to be seen again. We are all guilty of spending the tax savings provided by traditional IRA deductions.

401K Plans

I do have a word of caution when it comes to 401K plans. Most plans offer only a handful of rather stodgy mutual funds choices. You might be able to earn more than your employer matching by investing your money in an after tax investment. For example, employer matching has to be greater than $4,500 a year if you have an account worth $150,000 and can earn 3% or more in a $150,000 account invested elsewhere.

If employer matching totaled $3,000 a year then you only have to earn 2% more in that other account. You want to reward the portfolios that provide you with the best returns. If you have less than 12 investment choices in your 401K plans, it would be wise to ask your employer for more choices. Chances are good management is in the same plan and have your best interests at heart. At an employee meeting ask how many funds in the plan have 5 star Morningstar ratings?

So how do you manage investments inside your 401K plans? Easy, look up the symbol on Morningstar.com by entering the name of the fund or ask your benefits department to get you a list of symbols for the funds in the plan.

Once you have the symbols you can enter them onto your Microsoft Money 401K Watch List. As we have already learned, mutual fund portfolios make us money. The mutual fund manager picks stocks that meet the funds objective and then he or she leaves it up to Wall Street to price them. Basically, that is precisely what we are doing. It only takes 4-weeks before we will know which portfolio Wall Street likes best. The best performing portfolio in real time (4-weeks) earns the right to have a position in your account. It will be hard to find five really good mutual funds that Wall Street likes among only twelve mutual funds offered. Twelve choices are really not enough. The better 401K plans will offer 20 to 40 funds. With that many, you should be able to find five worthy investments among the various asset classes, Large Cap, Mid Cap, Foreign, Real Estate, Commodities, and Bonds.

If you change employers, I favor rolling your previous employer account to a self directed IRA. Using the entire universe of mutual funds and making all the investment decisions, you should grow the account faster. To do the best job of managing your own money, you need the ability to choose from a wide array of top performing mutual funds.

You can drive yourself nuts calculating what you will need for retirement instead of looking at the big picture of saving and investing for an early retirement. All my clients were extremely interested in the income that could be generated from their pension and investments if they had to retire tomorrow.

As you save by paying yourself first and grow your investment accounts each year, you can multiply your total pensions and investment accounts times .065 to check on the amount of retirement income that could be generated today. If your pension accounts total $175,000 and your personal investment accounts total $175,000 then multiply .065 times $350,000 and you get $22,750. If your budget is $47,500 then you are 5 to 7 years from retirement. Just divide $47,500 by .065 to get the amount needed of $730,769.23 and look at the doubles needed to get you to that amount. What is most important is for you to continue saving money and managing it effectively.

No discussion about retirement would be complete without a word or two on investing in your company's stock inside your 401K plans. When all those Enron employees lost all their 401K money in 2001, I had little sympathy for them. Investing all their money in Enron stock was a foolhardy amateur mistake. It was even worse than amateur, it was just plain dumb. Many had an account worth more than a million dollars and they got greedy and lost it all. If they had a Certified Financial Planner working for them they would not have lost all their money. Most could have retired when their company went out of business if they had only been diversified.

So let me ask you my test question. How many mutual funds do you need to own in a retirement portfolio? The answer is FIVE. Even if one of the five were Enron stock, they would not have lost it all. One last point, the price of Enron stock fell steadily over the last year of its life. Can you imagine holding onto a loser for an entire year? They only had one horse hooked up to their financial wagon and it died.

Since it's beginning in 1935, Social Insecurity as I call it continues to be a very popular program among retirees. To qualify for retirement income benefits that can start as early as age 62, you have to work 40 quarters or 10 years. Quarters do not have to be with the same employer or consecutive. Married spouses can collect their earned Social Security benefit or ½ of their spouses whichever is greater. Benefits are adjusted each year for inflation. The Social Security Administration says payments to retirees amount to 40% of their monthly budget. Today we have three Americans working to pay for one Social Security recipient.

MANAGE YOUR OWN MONEY

A Retiree's Worst Nightmare

One of the biggest mistakes retirees make is relying solely on the stock market for all their monthly income. In years when the stock market produces no return at all, retired investors are forced to live on principle alone. Retirees interested in an abundant and steady income have to deal with financial advisors who sometimes sell investments that don't produce any income at all. Couple that with bad investment decisions and their unwillingness to adjust your exposure to equities in a down market and you have a recipe for Financial Failure.

Selling shares for monthly income is the opposite of Dollar Cost Averaging. You sell more shares when the market is down and fewer shares when the market is up. Your average share cost is higher than the price of the average share sold.

The workaround for this problem is to use the Predictor to sell enough shares at market peaks that can provide monthly income over the nest 6 months to 9 months. In addition to that, I would like to suggest using a balanced asset allocation that would put 40 to 50% of assets in bonds to provide a steady income uncorrelated to the stock market. It is unlikely that today's new retirees will have guaranteed monthly pension from their last employer. More than likely retirees will be transferring assets out of a 401k plan to an IRA account upon retirement. If the retiree were unable to manage a portfolio of bonds then an immediate annuity would be the best choice. I saw many of my retired clients make this mistake. All felt that it was easier to adjust their retirement income than to adjust their budget. Selling shares in a bear market for income is not a good idea. The best use of mutual funds in retirement is to provide income and a hedge against erosion of principle due to inflation. A retiree's worst enemy is inflation.

Are Retirement Annuities a good Idea?

Annuities are crafted and sold by insurance companies. Some grow at fixed interest rates determined by the company, these are called Fixed Annuities. Annuities that let you invest in mutual funds are called Variable Annuities. Annuities carry the promise to the owner of a lifetime income. Other settlement options include a monthly income for 5 years, 10 years, or for life with 10 years guaranteed, which is one of the more popular options.

There is no such thing as a complimentary annuity issued by a charitable organization and sold to the public by a group of volunteers. Annuities are very expensive to own, have huge penalties for early withdrawal called a Contingent Deferred Sales Charge (CDSC), and are sold for all the wrong reasons. I personally don't care for products that allow the agents to select the commission they wish to make. The longer the Contingent Deferred Sales Charge runs, the larger the concession to the dealer, and commission to the agent. Variable Annuities can have management and expense charges of 4% or more before you make a penny. If you have to own an annuity insist on one with no Contingent Deferred Sales Charge. That way if you don't like it for any reason, you can take your money and run without incurring a heavy penalty. How long do these penalties last? The larger the commission paid to the agent the longer the penalty for early withdrawal. The typical CDSC runs 7 years and pays the agent around 5% commission based on the amount invested, which would be $5,000 per $100,000 was invested.

Gains inside non-qualified annuities are tax deferred until money is withdrawn. Monthly annuity payments are broken down into two parts. Principal or the amount invested is not taxed. Interest or gain in a Variable Annuity is taxed as ordinary income. A single withdrawal is considered interest or gains and taxed as ordinary income. LIFO as we call it is last in, in this case interest, and is the first to come out.

Many people say, "Well, if you put a tax sheltered IRA into a tax deferred annuity you are putting a tax shelter inside a tax shelter." That might be true, but they are missing the point. Annuities are all about life incomes. You can't get a guaranteed income for life from an IRA. But, why pay all the fees if you don't have to? You can always purchase an Immediate Annuity when you are ready for a guaranteed life income that usually starts within 30 days.

The primary problem with annuities is that they are sold to the elderly who rarely need to defer taxes and for sure don't need a Contingent Deferred Sales Charge that can last 7 years or longer. Bonds would be a far better choice as they only pay a few hundred dollars in commissions. Most investors would be better off paying a low Commission to buy bonds.

Those over the age of 65 should only be interested in **Immediate Annuities** if income has to be guaranteed. Exchanging money for immediate payments is fine but there are more profitable places to invest your money like individual bonds.

One other benefit of an Immediate Annuity is that the income paid to the annuitant is protected from creditors. When someone purchases an Immediate Annuity, cash is exchanged for a monthly income for a period of years or for life.

Chapter 15

WAYS TO SAVE ON INSURANCE

Auto & Homeowners

Buying a personal auto or homeowners policy is no easy task but I will try to make it so. Property Casualty insurance companies insure our homes, cars, and businesses too. There is no need to harp on the need for insurance. What you need to know is the straight scoop. Are insurance agents acting in our best interest or theirs? All insurance companies have a hungry sales force that thrives on commissions and trips to Hawaii. We need to hold on to our wallet extra tight with both hands if they are in the middle of a sales contest. Insurance Agencies and agents may represent several insurance companies that might have minimum production requirements. You could be asked to buy a policy in order for them to meet a minimum production requirement. Insurance companies do put demands on agencies that sell their products. You never know what to expect when you walk through an insurance office door.

The fix for all this is to know the insurance company who has the best rates before you are invited into their office. You need to know what you want before you get there. In this modern age of computers and the Internet, consumers can shop for the best company with the best rates without walking through the front door of an insurance agency. It just took me a few clicks on Google to come up with a state Premium Study brochure.

I Googled **California Department of Insurance rates** and this came up:

http://www.insurance.ca.gov/0100-consumers/0060-information-guides/0040-residential/homeowner-premium-survey.cfm

Here is a link to Oregon's Department of Insurance:

http://insurance.oregon.gov/publications.html

I have not seen a state yet that did not publish a brochure on all the auto insurance companies admitted in that state and their rates in your neck of the woods. Once you have found the top two companies with the lowest rates you can go to their website to learn more and to see a list of the agencies selling their policy in your state and city. When you walk through their door, you will already know what company or companies you are interested in discussing.

A good agent will show you a couple of different deductibles. Your first reaction might be to go for the lowest deductible. The biggest savings in premium comes when you move the deductible from $250 to $500. Electing a $1,000 deductible only saves a little bit more. If you save the difference in premiums between those two deductible plans in a separate savings account, you will have the equivalent of a zero deductible policy in two to three years. So it makes sense to select the policy with the $500 deductible in order to bank the difference.

When I was doing financial plans for a fee, I told prospective clients that savings realized from my recommended changes would more than cover the cost of their financial plan. Fiddling with deductibles on their insurance was one way in which I did just that. This idea alone will cover the cost of this book and then some.

You can do the same with your homeowners insurance. Take the $500 deductible and reserve the savings so you eventually have a zero deductible. You are welcome to add as many bells and whistles on your auto and homeowners policies as you want. **My only concern is that you get the best policy at the best rates.** I do favor replacement cost riders that pay for loses without subtracting for depreciation, the HO5 homeowner's policy that extends full coverage to personal possessions, and uninsured motorists on your auto insurance policy. You might want coverage for earthquakes, floods, and other acts of Mother Nature based on risks in your area.

Driving the speed limit to avoid tickets is the best thing you can do to insure low rates on your auto insurance. Avoid distractions like your cell phone. If you want to save some big money, slow down so a full tank of gas can take you further down the road. Keeping your car longer will lower your cost per mile.

Life Insurance

Life insurance has many valid uses. Replacing economic value is well worth a modest term insurance premium. Replacing income lost when a breadwinner dies is one of the most important uses of life insurance. Multiples of salary is an easy way to buy more life insurance through an employer group life plan. An employee making $50,000 a year can elect to buy three to five times that amount through their employer. Ever increasing premiums is a drawback as they are banded in five-year increments based on one's age. I personally favor 10, 15, 20-year level premium term insurance, or decreasing term. As your estate grows ever larger, coverage can be decreased. Most life insurance agents believe that you should have life insurance until you die. For the moderately wealthy, that is not always the case. Estate taxes are not a problem for this group or loss of income. Larger estates might be concerned about preserving an estate. Funding a living trust can be done with insurance for small estates.

For businesses, there is Key Man life insurance to find and replace a valued executive. Companies need to be indemnified for loss of revenue caused by the untimely death of its president. Funding a buy-sell agreement is the perfect use of life insurance among business owners of partnerships and closely held corporations. I do believe in life insurance for all these reasons but I am not sure it will be needed until you die. Term insurance is undersold because the premium and agent compensation is so low. Insurance company budgets are geared up to run on a premium gasoline called Whole Life.

Insurance companies set aside some of the premium each year called reserves to pay the claim no matter which type of insurance you own. The difference is the contract owner owns the Whole Life reserves where the insurance company owns the term insurance reserves.

Money going into Whole Life that pays a dividend each year or a Universal Life policy that invests reserves in mutual funds is laden with to many layers of management fees and expenses. If the need is not permanent the product of choice should be term insurance. If the insurance has to be in force at death, Level Premium Term to age 100 might be the best choice. It is priced lower than a Whole Life policy yet higher than other renewable term insurance where the premium increases with age. An investment is not insurance nor is insurance an investment. Maybe that is why Universal Life never made a lot sense to me.

How much life insurance do you need in a family setting? My rule of thumb is half your income for 10 years. Take a person making $75,000 a year, a 7% return on insurance proceeds of $375,000 will pay the widow or widower $28,128.43 a year for 40 years! The deceased consumed about 35% of the budget so that is just about right. At 7% interest, a widow could expect $40,000 a year for 25.16 years. Plus, there are other benefits like Social Security survivor benefits if there were children. The death benefit on Social Security is a whopping $255. What kind of benefit is that?

At one time, I believed strongly that a permanent form of life insurance such as Whole Life served clients best. As I advanced in my career, I saw clients Net Worth exceed their need for insurance they had purchased to replace lost income in the event of death. For disciplined investors, Decreasing Term Life would have been the best product as retirement assets grew to replace the yearly drop in term insurance coverage. The only real problem I have with large life insurance premiums is that it diverts money away from our best investments. The Net Worth needed to fund our retirement will come from our investments not from our life insurance.

There is no such thing as a complimentary insurance policy issued by a charitable organization and sold to the public by a group of volunteers! A delivery system based on commissions and agency overrides is a very expensive delivery system. That is why premiums are so high. Companies and their agents operate on revenue generated by cash value life insurance. Current compensation can run from 50% of the first year premium to 100% or more of the first year premium.

The life insurance industry is still guilty of wholesale replacement of other company's products. The only way to end that bad behavior is to level agent compensation and make compensation transferable to a servicing agent chosen by the policyholder.

No current policy in force should be cancelled or replaced until underwriting approves your application for new insurance.

Chapter 16

CREATING YOUR ESTATE PLAN

Ways to Distribute Property at Death

There are many ways to distribute property at death. Property can pass through **title,** joint ownership, the law of contracts, and through a Will or Trust.

Dying Without a Will

In the absence of a Will or Trust, the <u>Intestate Laws</u> of the state in which you live will decide how your property is distributed.

Married with no children – Half would go to the surviving spouse and half to the deceased spouse's parents.

Married with one child – Half to the surviving spouse and half to the child at age 18.

Married with two or more children – 1/3 to the surviving spouse and 2/3 to the children at age 18.

No matter how a Will is written, it only takes two witnesses to make it legal.

Wills go through a full probate as long as the estate is above the states minimum size. Probate Court is not interested in probating very small estates. Call your nearest Probate Court to find out the minimum size in your state. Sometimes that minimum size changes year-to-year. The cost of probate, court and attorney's fees, is approximately 5% on the Gross Estate, which would include the full fair market value of the family residence.

Will a Will Work

A Will is nothing more than a **letter of instruction** stating who gets your property at your death. It also instructs the executor to pay off all your bills, which include taxes, medical expenses, and debt. It also names who gets your most prized possessions. The I love you his and her Wills simply state, "When I die, I leave all my worldly goods to my husband." The husband's Will says, "When I die, I leave all my worldly goods to my wife." They can be holographic, written by hand, crafted by an attorney, or you can buy software that will produce a written document to sign. There is one really big problem with relying on Wills alone to distribute your property. Surviving spouses have been known to remarry and die leaving all their assets to their new husband or new wife. Eventually that spouse dies and leaves all his or her worldly property to his or her children and not the children of the spouse that was first to die. Wills all by themselves are no guarantee you will inherit anything. I have even seen spouses change their will after the first spouse dies. What you once agreed to in marriage may not be what happens in the end.

When you Need a Will There is a Way

I say you are never too old to have a Will. The minute you have something you would like to leave someone at your death is a very good time to draft your first Will, which can be as simple as a holographic or hand written Will witnessed by **two parties over the age of 18**. Judges do like to see addresses of the two witnesses. Absent of that, the minute someone throws rice into your hair, you need a Will. Once you slip that ring over the finger of a significant other, you need a Will.

Marriage is a merger of two people and their assets. In most states it is called Common Law Property. Common Law Property holds that your spouse has legal right to claim a fair and equitable portion of your property in divorce.

A Prenuptial Agreement in a common law property state can list property owned prior to the marriage as sole and separate property in the event of divorce. You have to be very careful that both parties were **properly represented** during the crafting of any Prenuptial Agreement.

In Community Property States, whatever you bring into the marriage or receive through gifts or inheritances remains yours, but whatever you earn or acquire during the marriage is co-owned by both parties, regardless of who's name is on the title or who earned it.

Per Capita or Per Stirpes

You will need to decide if you wish to distribute your property Per Capita or Per Stirpes. If a named beneficiary in your Will or Trust predeceases you, would you want that person's share go to their children? If the answer is yes, then you wish your property be distributed Per Stirpes. If the answer is no, then you wish your property be distributed Per Capita. If a beneficiary predeceases you and you want their share to be divided among the other beneficiaries equally, then you wish your property be distributed Per Capita. Are grandchildren a requirement in order to distribute property Per Stirpes? No, it can be written if there is issue (children of the deceased) otherwise Per Capita.

Chapter 17

DESIGNING YOUR TRUST TO LAST

A Trust is nothing more than another kind of **letter of instruction** that simply names the beneficiaries of your estate, when, and how they are to receive distributions from the trust. A Trust gives title to all your property including personal property. You are called the Trustmaker; in fancy legal mumbo jumbo the operative word is Grantor, the person who made the trust. Let's keep things simple okay? So we have one pot of money now titled in the name of the trust. Prior to the trust, assets were held in Joint Tenancy. Acting as trustees of all your assets, you can still buy, sell, and do all the things you did with your property prior to signing trust documents. You simply add TTEE to the end of your legal signature. A trust's title that I like best reads like this, "Matthew Doe, trustee and Mary Doe, trustee of the Doe Living Trust dated May 18, 2008". There are several worthwhile benefits to having a trust and they are:

- Assets pass outside of Probate Court saving court and attorney's fees of 5% and a years worth of delay
- It drastically reduces Estate Taxes and in many cases eliminates inheritance taxes altogether
- Assets can be held and managed in a trust for the life of the beneficiary plus 21 years
- Distribution of property is private
- You can't be disinherited if you are the beneficiary of a Trust
- Allows for the professional management of trust assets
- Assets held in a trust don't belong to the beneficiary so they are not included in divorce settlements

Wills have their place in planning but both a Will and Trust is a good idea once you have an estate of $150,000 or more. I was privileged to work with Jim Hicks, a wonderful attorney in Flint, Michigan, for more than a decade. He knew how to plan better than anyone else on the planet. I will be forever grateful for what Jim taught me, all of which I am going to share with you now. Here are some of the options you have when it comes to crafting your Trust.

Would you want a provision in your trust that would stop income payments in the event the surviving spouse remarries? Yes, you can do that if you want.

College Incentives

A. All costs of college to an accredited university could be paid by the trust.

B. If the student's grade point average is better than 3.5 then they could withdraw a specified sum of say $3,000. Get a 4.0 and you get $5,000. An incentive for getting good grades is proper use of a financial carrot!

C. Upon receiving a bachelor's degree from an accredited university, you can withdraw $15,000 or you can select a different amount.

Would you want to allow a special withdrawal for a daughter's first time marriage?

I don't know how many times I asked this question over the years but wives have won this one each time every time. There is usually very little discussion on this issue. Their answer was always **yes** and wives always picked a greater amount of money to pay for the marriage and often added money for the honeymoon. As I recall, no wife ever lost to a husband when it came to providing a generous amount of money to make a wedding more memorable with beautiful flowers and lace.

Would you want to help provide part of the down payment on a son or daughter's first home purchase?

Here you can specify a part of the down payment in the form of a percentage to a maximum dollar amount. For example you might say, "A withdrawal of 50% of the down payment can be made to help with the first home purchase to a maximum of $40,000." This was very popular with my clients.

Ways to pay principal from a trust?

It is customary to distribute income earned by a trust. You can instruct the trustee to pay out a certain percentage of the trust and if the earnings are not sufficient instruct the trustee to add principal if necessary. Income can be paid monthly, quarterly, semi-annually, or annually.

There are many good reasons not to distribute 100% of the proceeds from a trust in a lump sum. The inability to manage trust assets and handing money over to a son or daughter-in-law in the event of divorce are two. There are several ways of distributing principal from a trust and the most popular are:

- 1/3 at age 30, 1/3 at age 35, and 1/3 at age 40
- 25% at age 30, 35, 40, and 45

Because beneficiaries usually know so little about investing, unless they read this book, I would opt to have the money kept in trust with monthly income for life, especially if they don't manage money well. Another option along those lines would provide an income for life and 21 additional years divided equally among the grandchildren. One client did not want her two sons to have access to trust principal until they were 55, which took me by surprise.

Chapter 18

HOW TRUSTS WORK

Are Trusts easy to manage?

Yes, they really are. Trusts are all about title. When both husband and wife are living, you have one trust title. When one of them dies it is just a matter of dividing trust assets in half lending a new title to the newly created trust "The John Doe Marital Trust dated May 18, 2020". Trusts are not to be feared because the deceased's trust can pay for all the care of the survivor down to the last penny. What beneficiary's can't do is rush down to the Successor Trustee home or office asking for all the money. A surviving spouse can withdraw 5% or $5,000 whichever is greater in any given year.

The cost of a Trust

In my 30-year career, I saw some very expensive trusts costing upwards of $5,000 or more and I have seen some very inexpensive trusts done for under $1,000. I have never seen where paying more gets you more. You already know all that trusts can do from this chapter. There is software available that can print a basic trust but I am not sure all that we have talked about here would be included in the trust. Attorneys use software to generate trusts too but I doubt many of the provisions discussed here would be in their software package leaving much to be done by hand. Get your quotes first!

Who selects the successor trustee?

There is one provision of a trust that I really like and that is the ability of the beneficiary to change the Successor Trustee if they are unhappy with the acting trustee, usually a bank trust department. Clients were encouraged to name an **institution** such as a bank trust department as the successor trustee but felt it was important to let the beneficiary pick another commercial trust department if they were unhappy for any reason. It does keep trust departments working in the beneficiary's best interest. Plus, institutions have been known to ask the beneficiary to select another trustee.

Can a beneficiary be named as successor trustee?

Yes, they can **but** they are usually not good at managing trust assets. Not knowing much about distributions from trusts, they might inadvertently ignore Limited Powers of Appointment and make the decedents trust taxable for Estate Tax purposes. Limited Powers of Appointment provide the <u>necessities of life in reasonable comfort</u>. I personally favor an independent third party trustee. Another reason is that it prevents bickering by beneficiaries and boy do they love to bicker.

Trust Design - Are Attorneys Savvy?

Those that specialize, yes, for the majority regretfully, the answer is no. I hope this chapter will fall into the hands, and be read, by Estate Planning attorneys so they can get crafty when it comes to client distribution choices outlined in this chapter. The other thing I would ask of all attorneys is to spend more time with clients. In a mad rush to get things done too much can be overlooked. Give clients their money's worth and spend some time with them. You will make clients happy and they will reward you with more referrals.

As stated earlier, trusts do not have to go through probate. One of the benefits of a trust is that they avoid the long probate process required for wills alone. Having said all this, it was customary for me in my practice to read client trusts. I was reading through one and found a provision to take the trust to probate. My eyes just about popped out of my head. You will never guess who was selected to be the attorney to probate the trust. Clients were more than willing to let me read their trust so I could look for dubious language such as this. When working with attorneys, I always asked for a copy to make sure everything the client wanted was included.

Do Banks Know Enough About Trusts?

Bank's trust departments do know about trusts because many act as trustees. The problem with banks today is that they are only looking for the large trusts with large amounts of money. Don't be afraid to talk to some of the smaller banks where trust size is less. Small institutions might give better service and perhaps even produce superior returns on invested assets. There are some trust companies that will trustee as little as $250,000. My best recommendation is to get on the Internet and Google "Trust Companies." Glean what you can from their website and give them a call to ask about fees, track record, and minimum trust size. Fees typically run one to two percent of assets under management depending on the amount of money in the trust.

Reviewing Your Trust

If you read all the above before you crafted your trust, you would see that every year it is worth a short discussion. When your economic circumstances change, your trust should be reviewed. Relationships with beneficiaries change, beneficiary's circumstances change, and relationships with grandchildren may change. Should you decide to add or subtract a beneficiary or wish to change how money is distributed it is time for your First Amendment. If a trustee can no longer act as trustee and no secondary trustee remains, it is time to craft an amendment naming a new successor trustee. Reviewing your trust once a year is recommended. Seeing an attorney periodically will make sure you don't overlook anything.

Basic Estate Planning Documents

- Revocable Living Trust – This document avoids Probate and reduces estate taxes
- Certification of Trust – A shortened copy of the necessary pages of the trust used to title assets in the name of the trust
- Asset Schedule – Lists the assets to be owned by the trust
- Pour-over Wills – Transfers assets held outside the trust to the trust upon death
- Community Property Agreement – Changes title from Joint Tenancy to Community Property
- Transfer Documents – Letters of instruction to institutions asking title be changed to the trust
- General Durable Power of Attorney – Authorizes another person to pay bills upon the incapacity of the trustee
- Durable Power of Attorney for Health Care Decisions – Authorizes another person to make health care decisions, usually a family member
- Directive to Physicians – Authorizes termination of life support systems
- Distribution of Personal Property – Provides a place to name a beneficiary of personal property
- Other – Special Instructions to the trustee, instructions for funding the trust, and guidelines for trustees upon death

Attorney Judith Bohlander, whom I worked with while in private practice, first introduced the above Estate Planning Documents to me. Over the years, I modified them slightly to read easier for clients.

The last thing you need do is file for is a tax ID number for the decedent's trust.

Chapter 19

MISCELLANEOUS THOUGHTS ABOUT MONEY

Stop loss orders – Many investors draw a line in the sand by putting a stop loss sell order under the purchase price of their investment. Professional traders know you do that and love to drive the market down by shorting stock or an index. The investment is stopped out and sold for a loss. Investors are dazed and stunned that this could have happened as they watch the price climb right back up to where it was before the sudden drop. How could this happen to my favorite stock and me, they ask? Well, the professional trader can profit by selling the stocks they don't own, which is called shorting the stock, and then taking advantage of the lower price to cover their short and then they get long quickly as the price rises. Seeing the price recover those automatically stopped out buy it back driving the price even higher.

Then the professional traders sell posting a nice profit to their account at your expense. Stop loss orders, when triggered, are always a guaranteed loss. This is just one more reason I like mutual fund investing over the ownership of individual stocks. These down drafts can happen over the course of a whole day or can last for a few seconds intra-day, down hard one day and up hard the next. I pay little attention to what happens in a single days worth of trading on Wall Street.

Story stocks and rumors – Parties are the last place on earth to find new investment ideas. Stories get exaggerated and embellished when told under the influence of alcohol. Everyone has a story about his or her favorite stock. Rumors are just a story whispered into ones ear. It is just another form of hype told differently. Smart investors stay away from stories, rumors, and institutional hype.

Investment time horizon – Investment failure is caused by impatient investors not giving their investments enough time to produce a profit. The investor stays in the investment just long enough to show a loss and then they sell. The best time to get long is at the end of magenta crossing the − 100 line. When you don't enter a trade at the proper time, often you have to take a little heat until price can get you into the green. If you read the book you know what green I am talking about.

Limited Partnerships are an expensive business form that I have never liked. In a Limited Partnership, your risk is limited to the amount of money invested. Tax write-offs are passed through to the limited partners on K-1 statements that arrive in March of each year. There are real estate, oil and gas drilling partnerships, and equipment leasing partnerships to name a few where tax write-offs are passed through to limited partners. The reasons I don't care for investing in Limited Partnerships is there is a lack of liquidity if you have to sell. They can drive you nuts during a holding period of 10 to 15 years. You have no say in the business. A General Partner justified over spending his construction budget by saying, "Limited Partners are accustomed to losing money."

Manage Your Own Money "To Do" List

- Acquire and install a version of Microsoft Money
- Set up your current accounts on Microsoft Money
- Set up your portfolio columns with moving averages
- Search Morningstar.com for top performing funds
- Enter funds onto your various Watch Lists
- Setup and save the Predictor at Stockcharts.com
- Practice by paper-trading the Predictor
- Craft your budget
- Do your first balance sheet
- Review your retirement accounts
- Create a plan in your budget to reduce debt to zero
- Review your auto and homeowners insurance
- Review your life insurance
- Review and discuss your Will and Trust
- Set short and long-term financial goals
- Pick your path to prosperity and stick to it
- Set up meetings to discuss your financial situation
- Upload daily Wall Street closing prices into Microsoft
- Add new websites to your favorites folder
- Save this book for future reference

Thank you for letting me help you
Manage Your Own Money!

With warm regards,

Daniel J. Clemons

My Favorite Money Websites

Mrs. Marlo Zeller, a business and health teacher at the Rogue Valley Youth Correctional Facility, has a blog on my Personal Money Management Course here:

http://personalmoneymanagementcourse.blogspot.com/

You can stay abreast of the market intra-day here:

http://biz.yahoo.com/mu/update.html

Zacks Investment Research will email a Free Newsletter of stocks they like upon request here:

http://www.zacks.com/

Technical Analysis can also be found here:

http://www.stockta.com/cgi-bin/analysis.pl?symb=&num1=5&cobrand=&mode=stock

Here is an interesting birthday calculator:

http://www.paulsadowski.com/birthday.asp

This is the home page on my computer:

http://clearstation.etrade.com/

Financial Fun Quiz

1. How much money should you have in an Emergency Fund?

    A. Three months income.

    B. Enough to pay your bills for six months.

    C. An amount equal to your expenditures for two months.

    D. Emergency funds are not necessary when you have a retirement plan through your employer.

2. Your best friend wants to lower investment risk. You advise them to:

    A. Adjust their Asset Allocation.

    B. Diversify their risk away by investing in more conservative mutual funds.

    C. Put more money into Bond Mutual Funds.

    D. Stop reading the financial pages of their local newspaper.

3. The primary reason for financial failure is

    A. Excessive amount of debt.

    B. Inability to spend less than they make.

    C. Divorce caused by a midlife crisis.

    D. Lack of a financial plan.

    E. All of the above.

4. **The rule of 72 means**

    A.   Some younger people with not collect Social Security until they are age 72.

    B.   Divide an interest rate into 72 and it tells you how long it will take for your money to double.

    C.   Divide the number of years into 72 and it tells you how much interest you have to earn to double your money.

    D.   Once you reach age 72, you no longer have to pay taxes on your Social Security.

    E.   B and C only.

5. **Your younger brother who is 24 tells you that he would like to start an IRA next year. Your advice to him is**

    A. Congratulations on your wise decision. Next year sounds great!

    B. No problem, you still have 41 years to save for retirement.

    C. If you don't start it this year you will have $48,068.01 less in your account at age 65.

    D. Better to put half in this year and half in next year than to wait one year.

6. Your sister knows you read Manage Your Own Money. She's now looking to you for financial advice and she asks you, "What should I invest in first?" Your advice is

    A.   To invest in your company 401K plan.

    B.   Come see me when your credit cards are paid in full.

    C.   When you get $2,500 saved, come see me and we'll pick a good mutual fund for you.

    D.   You need a new car before you begin investing.

7. The biggest mistake small investors make is:

    A. They don't save regularly

    B. They sell their mutual funds when their account value falls below the amount they invested.

    C. Letting human emotions make their investment decisions.

    D. Relying on Money Magazine articles for sound investment advice.

    E. All of the above

8. The best way to save on your income taxes is to:

    A.   Invest in Tax Free Municipal Bonds.

    B.   Invest in a Qualified Retirement Plan.

    C.   Invest in Tax Credit Programs.

    D.   Invest in a non-qualified Tax Deferred Annuity.

Answers

1. **A-Three month's income** is needed to fund your budget during periods of unemployment or other short-term financial need.

2. **A-Adjust their Asset Allocation** by taking money out of funds with a high standard deviation.

3. **All of the above.**

4. **B and C only**

5. **C is the correct answer.** The cost of waiting to invest is high.

6. **I believe you should eliminate your debt first.**

7. **The biggest amateur mistake is buying at the top of markets and selling at the bottom. They think they are going to lose all their money so they let human emotion make their decisions.**

8. **B of course.**

In Summary

No one cares more about your money than you do. Investors look at their accounts more often than the institutions that hold their money. Investors care about returns while Broker Dealers care more about commissions. The cost of managing your money should be less as a result of a good financial education. You have all the tools you need to pick mutual funds better than a broker because you know how to set up and use a Watch List. In front of my high school seniors, I always raise my right hand and promise that in six to seven short classes they will know how to manage their money better than any financial institution in any state. I know that is a strong statement but I know what a Series 7 licensed Registered Representative knows and I know what they don't know. I know what a Certified Financial Planner knows and I know what they don't know. If you have read this book, you now know more then they know when it comes to portfolio construction and the investment selection process. You know more about Technical Analysis then they do. You own The Predictor and they don't. You know how to save on your insurance. I have given you Paths to Prosperity you will read nowhere else. You know how to craft your trust to do more things for the people you love and care about most.

No part of my money management technology that I used professionally in private practice has been left out of this book. Everything discussed herein is true to the best of my knowledge and I thank you from the bottom of my heart for buying and reading my book. There is nothing more I can say or do to help you Manage Your Own Money any better.

Acknowledgements

Special thanks goes to my wife Vickie Clemons for inspiring me to write this book. She has always wanted to know more about how to manage our investments if something should happen to me. Vickie skillfully helped to edit this book.

I would like to thank Marlo Zeller, an excellent business teacher in the Three Rivers School District, for meticulously editing every single page in this book. Marlo made a **major contribution** and I very much appreciate her help and expertise.

Challenging me often is my very good friend of 26 years, Bill Porter, for suggesting titles and encouraging me to explain topics in greater detail. Bill's company Lumen Systems, Inc. writes Financial Planning software for investment professionals so his financial brain works really well. Thank you, Bill.

Karl Messmore, a close friend and business associate of many years, was the first person to ever read this book. Insurance is his area of expertise so he offered some food for thought that made it into the book. Karl, I thank you.

Thanks to my two brothers in law: Mark and Vernon Pilkington who shared some of their concerns about money they wanted to see addressed in the book. Thanks to both of you.

Thanks to Sherman and Marian McClellan for use of their McClellan Summation Index, which was first presented in their book, *Patterns for Profit* (available from McClellan Financial Publications).

Hugs to my beautiful granddaughter Amber R. Shively for writing the title to Chapter 14.

This book would not be possible without the cooperation of Stockcharts. com. I have been a subscriber to their services for a very long time. I tip my financial hat to Chip Anderson for allowing me to include his beautiful charts in this book.

Please know that I have no economic ties to the institutions mentioned in this book other than those specifically mentioned such as Zions Direct. I do own all the Mutual Funds mentioned in this book except BURKX and have received zero compensation for mentioning their names. I am long MTW and GS and showed them to you because they both had an interesting chart. Don't get all excited about what I own because I could have sold it by the time you read this. All the views expressed are mine and do not reflect the views of any individual, mutual fund company or institution mentioned in the book. I am no longer a licensed professional in private practice. I am retired and no longer a practicing Certified Financial Planner.

In March 2007, my principal forwarded an email from Dan Clemons who was requesting an opportunity to present his Personal Money Management Course to our high school students. I was hesitant at first but his material looked most intriguing so I decided to let him teach one of his six part Personal Money Management Course classes. The students and I found Dan interesting, motivating, inspiring, exciting, knowledgeable, and a true professional dedicated to helping young adults make better decisions about their money. Classes frequently ended with applause and students were eager to shake his hand and learn more. "This is the best class I have ever taken," one student expressed as he walked out the door.

It is now 2008 and students and staff alike love to attend Dan's classes. With each passing class, I see our student's faces light up with confidence as they learn to **Manage Their Own Money.**

Marlo Zeller
Business Teacher, Newbridge High School, Grants Pass, OR

4213230

Made in the USA
Lexington, KY
06 January 2010